Killing for God

By Dr. Paul Kamble

January 21, 2016

By
Dr. Paul Kamble

January 21, 2016

Printed through:
CreateSpace
an Amazon Company

CONTENTS

FOREWORD

This is not a book, this is an encyclopedia, a mini-encyclopedia, if you will. If it were an institution, it would be a small university with an assortment of departments. What is unique about this magnum opus, though, is that it is one man's work. And it shows the sweep of his knowledge, the depth of his erudition and the mettle of his commitment to Truth. Truth is as simple as black and white, but to tell the Truth, depending on its nature and content and also the circumstances in which it is told, can be a dangerous undertaking. The famous dictum: "In time of universal deceit, telling the truth is a revolutionary act." But to those who are committed to telling it as it is, no other option is available. So I congratulate Dr. Kamble for venturing into a minefield of misunderstanding, criticism and possible hostile reactions. He assures us that as a Christian living under the precept of loving friends and foes alike, he harbors malice for none and good will for all.

Dr. Kamble is a historian, a sociologist, an economist, a meticulous researcher credited with talent, enthusiasm and painstaking effort. Above all, he is a versatile scholar with the divine gift of curiosity. Among the topics he has discussed in this collection of essays, a prominent section is devoted to various aspects of Islamic studies.

It is safe to say that in America, even among fairly well educated citizens, there is a conspicuous absence of curiosity when it comes to what anthropologist, Ruth Benedict calls "Other Cultures." Some years ago while I was doing post graduate studies at Delhi School of Economics, an

American missionary asked me if I could give a talk to the American Embassy families on Buddhism. I never suspected that my audience would turn out to be 8th graders!

Even after the nine/eleven tragedy in which nineteen Muslim radicals commandeered four airplanes full of Americans and used them as guided missiles to destroy America's pride, Americans haven't tried enough to understand what Islam is capable of and what irrational behaviors Islamic sources can inspire in some of its followers. Dr. Kamble's research published in this work should go a long way in educating the public of the rudiments of Islam.

As a teenager I grew up among Muslims. I have had enough contact with the "believers" to make proper distinction between Islam and Muslims. And my focus here, as it is that of Dr. Kamble, is Islam and not individual Muslims. I know from my limited experience and fairly wide reading, that there are millions and millions of Muslims who are decent and peace-loving human beings, caring, compassionate and kind. V.S. Naipaul during his travels "Among the Believers" came across also Muslims who called themselves "Statistical Muslims," slack in their practice of the faith, but rattled by the violence perpetrated by some of their fellow Muslims who bring discredit to the community which is called in Arabic "Umma." Naipaul speaks about Arab Imperialism in which the Arabs, particularly, Saudi Arabia tries to impose its own brand of Islam by pouring billions of dollars into the Wahhabi brainwashing machine called madrassas. Naipaul writes: "Islam almost from the start, had been an imperialism as well as a religion, with an early history remarkably like a speeded-up version of the history of Rome, developing from city-state to peninsular overlord, to empire, with corresponding stresses at every stage." (Among the Believers P.7)

Among today's believers, two broad divisions can be identified: An overwhelming majority of peace loving, law abiding and observant Muslims (who make Islam a religion of peace) and a violent, radicalized fringe that makes Islam look like the Empire of Tamerlane.

Indeed, divisions have existed and still exist in other religions as well. Christianity is one clear example of divisions – the fault line running all the way through the Middle Ages - but they could be mended by going back to the sources where the means for mending the cracks have been provided: "Love thine enemies." Christian teaching provides us the intelligence and humility to realize, as in Shakespeare's Julius Caesar, that "the faults are not in our stars, dear Brutus, but in ourselves." In Islam, however, there are no such provisions in its sources, instead, we see a widening rift between groups such as Shias and Sunnis. Muslim journalist Hasan Suroor writes in Hindu (September 29, 2014) that "the Koranic text is a minefield of ambiguity allowing people to cherry-pick equivocal and often contradictory verses to back their arguments." Further on, in the same article, Suroor quotes a distinguished British Pakistani Islamic scholar (Ziauddin Sardar) "There is no denying the streak of violence which is "inherent" in Islam." So peace and hostility coexist in the same Islamic sources which they all recite yet understand differently. Young Muslims are taught tolerance and peaceful coexistence in India, while In Pakistan and Saudi Arabia, they are taught Jews are pigs and Christians are monkeys and Islam is God 3.0, Christians are God 2.0, Jews are God 1.0 and Hindus and all others are God 0.0. The lessons are, alas, drawn from the same sources.

We face three major problems when we try to delve deep into the history and teaching of Islam: 1. Why did the immediate followers of Muhammad fail to bring about a smooth succession? What caused the Shia/Sunni divide? 2. After a thousand years of glory, what caused the humiliating fall of Islamic civilization? And 3. If the Koran is the literal word of Allah and co-eternal with him, what accounts for the baffling contradictions in the Koranic text?

1. When Islam's founder, Muhammad died suddenly in AD 632, there was no designated successor or a system of succession. During the powwow that ensued, two contestants emerged to claim leadership of the community. They based their claims on bloodlines. The first was Abu Bakr, a close friend of Muhammad and father of Aisha, Muhammad's favorite wife and a force to be reckoned with in her own right. The second contestant was Ali, Muhammad's cousin and husband of his daughter Fatimah. Plenty of bad blood had existed between Ali and Aisha before the question of succession came up. There was no love lost between Aisha and Khadija, Muhammad's first wife and Fatimah's mother. And also Aisha hated Ali for demanding punishment to be meted out to her for spending time with a young fighter who was not a relative. The story of the 'Lost Necklace' is well known in the history of Islam. Abu Bakr and Ali had

supporters in the community. The partisans of Abu Bakr were called 'Sunnis, for they decided to follow the 'Sunna' which is described as the code of pious practices based on Muhammad's example.

The supporters of Ali were called Shi'at Ali or the party of Ali from which the term Shia is derived. Abu Bakr was almost immediately chosen successor or Caliph because Aisha testified that Muhammad had designated him as the successor. When Ali was passed over two more times, his party rebelled. So he was made Caliph in 656. Ali's claim was, nonetheless, hotly contested. Intense hatred, spawned by the ever deepening family feud, played a role in the assassination of Ali at Kufa in 661 by an extremist whose poisoned sword struck a tragic note that has reverberated ever since. The Shia-Sunni schism pitted Muslim against Muslim and led to civil wars, massacres and collapse of dynasties. The split and its deadly consequence have lasted even to our own day with no effort at compromise or unity.

Pope Benedict XVI argued that for any move towards understanding and unity, the discussions should be based on reason. The Pope added that a conception of God without reason leads to violence. An effort was made in Basra and Bagdad, (Iraq) in the 8th century to build up an Islamic theology based on reason and rational thinking. The effort was masterminded by a group called the 'Mutazilites' who were inspired by Greek Philosophy and Christian Apologetics. Mutazilites denied the presumed status of the Koran as uncreated and co-eternal with God. Though the Abbasid Caliphate endorsed the Mutazilites position, it lasted only two centuries and was confined only to a small area in Iraq.

A New school of theology called the Asharites replaced the Mutazilite School. They contradicted and rejected the rationalist position of the Mutazilites. The primacy of reason lost out to the primacy of will and power. God was pure will. He can change his mind and do anything he wills. Asharites reinstated the status of the Koran as co-eternal with God. They taught that it is inscribed on a tablet in heaven and it appears exactly today in Arabic. Muhammad Ibn Zakariya a Razi, a Persian Polymath who lived between the years of 854 and 925 AD challenged this position. ".......... You claim that the evidentiary miracle is present and available, namely the Koran. You say: "Whoever denies it, let him produce a similar one." Indeed, we shall produce a thousand from the works of rhetoricians, eloquent speakers and valiant poets, which are more appropriately phrased and state the issues more succinctly. They convey the meaning better and their rhymed prose is in better meter.... By God, what you say astonishes us! You are talking about a work which recounts ancient myths, and which at the same time is full of contradictions and does not contain any useful information or explanation. Then you say: 'produce something like it." Contemporaries of Sheikh Zakariya a Razi referred to him as 'that infidel, that crazy ex-Muslim'. And the Sheikh retorted: "If the people of this religion are asked about proof of the soundness of their religion, they flare up, get angry and spill the blood of whoever confronts them with this question. They forbid rational speculation, and strive to kill their adversaries. This is why truth became thoroughly silenced and concealed."

The second dilemma, namely, what caused the collapse of the Islamic civilization after a thousand years of glory, has been effectively studied by the eminent Islamic scholar, Bernard Lewis, respected and endorsed by both Muslims and non-Muslims alike. In a tribute, the late Fouad Ajami said in 2006: "Bernard Lewis, the esteemed scholar of Islam and of the Middle East is one of the Cassandras of our time." Cassandra, by the way, was one of the princesses of Troy, astonishingly beautiful and blessed with the gift of foreseeing the future. Bernard Lewis in his book, "Clash of Civilizations" written way before the nine/eleven, refers to the 'tense dynamic between Islam and the West' and offers a historical case for what he calls the Muslim world's "downward spiral of hate and spite, rage and self-pity, poverty and oppression." And though, he does not explicitly mention it, he leaves his readers to ponder the question: whether a religion rooted in the belief that all truth was revealed to its prophet, can ever successfully embrace change.

The downward spiral of the Islamic civilization was set off with the military defeat at the gate of Vienna in 1683. The setback was repeated in other spheres as well when the Western (Christian) societies leaped ahead. Muslims tried to respond, but they conflated Westernization and Modernization together. They rejected Westernization, but sought modernization. Lewis says, 'it's a bleak roadmap of missteps to the Islamic world of today, impoverished in almost everything but terrorism and despotism.' Hasan Suroor whom I already quoted above, says: "There has been no Islamic equivalent of Enlightenment and Renaissance, and the Islamic mindset remains awkwardly out of step with historical progress, and therefore, with modern times, reinforced by attempt to assert an Islamic identity through beards and hijabs.

The third and the last question is how to reconcile the contradictions that exist in Islam with the stultifying claim that Islam is so perfect that there is nothing in it that needs change or reform. Some of the mainstream Muslims or the silent majority accept this position without questioning. They believe that there is no need for any reform in Islam. In most Muslim communities, the operational principle is: "yours is not to question why; yours is to do and die." Independent thinking is not encouraged, in fact, it is often stifled. Philosopher Susan Neiman defines an adult as a person who has developed a capacity for independent thinking, a talent that society conspires to stifle. Islamic societies, particularly the ones dominated by fundamentalist thinking, have conspired to stifle independent thinking. Most believers in those societies are so docile as to live with contradictions that exist in their religion, yet never question. They will tell you that Islam is a religion of peace and yet, watch without dismay the mindless violence that are often perpetrated in its name. They will tell you that women in their society enjoy equality and are treated with dignity and respect, and yet, they are aware of the fact that in Islam, a woman's testimony is only half as good as that of a man. They see no irony in the fact that their religion exhorts its followers to gain knowledge even if it means "going to China" yet, they condone killing of little girls for attending school. Their leaders preach tolerance and peaceful coexistence with other communities but they never ask why their religion is so often described as synonymous with hate and intolerance.

Hasan Suroor whom we have already met in these pages, admits that Islam has two faces: There are some Muslims who cite the Koran and the Hadith to underline injunctions against violence, and the command to respect women, and practice tolerance, love and brotherhood, but then there are also other Muslims like Taliban who quote the same sources to show the legitimacy of their positions on treating infidels and renegades the way they do.

Suroor tries to explain these conflicts by chalking them up to texts that lend themselves to misunderstanding and misinterpretation. He and many others like him have suggested ways of remedying the confusion, but these moderate, well- educated Muslims exert hardly any influence in the larger community. Any suggestion of change or reform is rejected outright, because "the Koran is the literal word of Allah revealed progressively to Prophet Muhammad." So moderate Muslims as well as non-Muslims are left with a bunch of questions with no convincing answers!

I feel it would be ungracious of me to end these comments on Islam's history on a pessimistic note. Islam has its problems just as other organized religions, but it would be grossly unfair to portray the second largest religion in the world as a problem in itself. Islam's contribution to world civilization and to progress in the sciences is enormous. The way it transformed Arab society is nothing less than phenomenal. Islam brought an end to 'Jahilliya' (period of ignorance); polytheism and widespread idolatry once practiced by the pre-Islamic Arabia were replaced by strict monotheism. Islam built some of the greatest cultures in the world and some of the world's great wonders. What happened to those powers, talents and the creative energy? Why has the once glorious civilization now ended up near the bottom of the heap? How did Islam get from Avicenna and Cordoba to Osama Bin Laden and the Al Qaeda? How does the strident call for jihad benefit the religion? The world today is too big and too powerful for one small group of

Jihadists to conquer and convert it to its own ideology. The world is moving inexorably forward and it is moving through cooperation and collaboration. Globalization is the language of mutuality and reciprocity. The rest of the world is moving towards unity, towards symbiosis.

As I write this, Pope Francis is addressing the United Nations. "You are a microcosm of the world," he reminded ambassadors of nations, "take care of each other. And if there are non-believers among you, I ask them to wish me well."

I have long understood that arguments never change hearts. As the great Indian sage, Kabir said, it is love that changes heart. So every morning I pray for a change of heart, first in me, and then in all the people who hate those who follow different ideologies. I wish Dr. Kamble much success in his effort to bring people together in wisdom and grace.

Joseph Devaprasad

INTRODUCTION

Rafiq Zakaria, Indian politician and Islamic scholar dedicated his book, "Muhammad and the Quran" to his two sons, Arshad and Fareed, students at Harvard and Yale. The dedication reads: "To my sons, Arshad and Fareed who wanted to have a Correct perception of the religion into which they have been born, so that they could Share the knowledge with their friends of Harvard and Yale, where misconceptions about Islam still persist. In the words of Benjamin Disraeli, they may have to 'learn to unlearn. 'The elder Zakaria, now no more, was right on the money when he said, "Misconceptions still persist." Misconceptions or ignorance about Islam has a much wider sweep than Harvard and Yale; they are almost everywhere in the country. I am not aware of what the Zakaria brothers have done to dislodge the ubiquitous mental disorder of ignorance. They are rich, influential, married to white American girls – an exciting part of the American Dream for many immerges – and live in the north-east. Fareed, the center of controversy last year, is a respected broadcaster for CNN. Fareed Zakaria GPS (Global Public Square) can be heard every Sunday morning. Fareed is reported to have acknowledged recently that he was not a religious person. So Zakaria brothers haven't helped, and misconceptions still persist.

There is no effective way we can deal with the Islamic world except through a thorough understanding of Islam and how it provokes the turbulence that rages through the world it inhabits. The emphasis on political correctness, so pervasive in our thinking, makes it all the more difficult for us to ask the right questions and get the right answers. Jonathan Chait writing in 'New York' magazine seems to think that political correctness is wildly out of control. What are the root causes of the malaise that poisons relation between the Islamic and non-Islamic worlds? That question has riled me for a long time, and I wanted to find the answer.

My search for the root causes of the conflict within Islam, and between Islam and others, has taken me all the way to the origin of Islam as set down in the original writings of Islamic scholars. Facts do not lie, so the objective of my research has been to uncover the facts as far as historically and humanly possible. I start my enquiry, therefore, with a disclaimer: As a true Christian open to the positive elements in other faiths, I have launched this enquiry with the sole purpose of unraveling the truth and exposing it without fear or malice. I have set before me the task of studying Islam, its history, its teaching, the Circumstances that expedited its rapid expansion and the causes of its negative perception throughout the world today. The angry young men and women like the quartet that committed murder and mayhem in the French capital on January 7, 2015 are not just a band of castaways of society seeking revenge for their perceived grievances. They are people with hope. They have been assured that their 'martyrdom' on this side of paradise would be richly rewarded with endless pleasure in the real paradise. This hope is what motivates them to kill and to die in the act of killing. The word 'martyrdom' in its original meaning is witnessing to one's own faith to the point of laying down his/her life. In other words, martyrdom is dying, not killing. Martyrdom is for heroes, not for cowards who flee after snuffing out innocent lives! Islam's use of the word 'martyrdom". Therefore, is a misuse of the term, just like its use of the word 'blasphemy!' Blasphemy in its real meaning is speaking profanely or irreverently against God or sacred things. It is an act of mocking divinity. Muhammad, Islam's founder never claimed to be divine. In fact, he insisted that he was only human like everyone else. So where do these ideas of martyrdom and blasphemy come from? My hunch is that it is a later misuse of terms borrowed from Judaism or Christianity. A critical analysis of Islam's history should, I believe, provide the real clue to the understanding of the terrorist mindset. And that is one of my reasons for undertaking this study. Creating a culture of hatred and death should be alien to the essential purpose of religion. The true purpose of religion is to create a culture of life and unity.

Freedom to Criticize

What Muslims must understand is that if they have the freedom to criticize the Bible, then other people have the same freedom to criticize the Quran.

Many Muslims feel that any criticism of the Quran is blasphemous and should not be allowed. This unrelenting attitude explains why Muslim apologists will not agree to debate the apparent errors and contradictions in the Quran. They want to debate the scriptures of other religions though, but never agree to debate their own scripture, the Quran.

No honest and open-minded discussion should be viewed as an attempt to belie or belittle a person's belief or the source of that belief. It should be taken as a sincere effort at understanding what is sacrosanct to the debaters. Hence discussions should be carried out in an objective and respectful manner so that they lead to the discovery of truth.

Any religion which refuses to allow people to examine its sacred books and long-held traditions using the normal rules of research and logic evidently has something to hide.

My aim in this essay is to undertake an analytical and critical study of Islam without any prejudice or subjective slant. I have conducted extensive research for more than two decades on the various aspects of Islam. I am a seeker, not a bigot. My aim is truth, not slander. This writer had the opportunity to speak about Islam in many places. So I prepared extensive notes and many like-minded individuals wanted to see my notes in a book format. I thank Almighty God for enabling me to present my research and study to the public in book form.

After 9/11, when thousands of innocent people were killed by Islamic extremists, the naive and historically ignorant American liberals began to ask "why do they hate us". “What is wrong with American Foreign Policy?” “America might have provoked the Islamic world". But the relevant question must be "what is wrong with the Islamic world, and why doesn’t it reform itself like Christianity and Hinduism". The basic problem is very clear: people in the Islamic world do not believe in free speech, freedom of religion, democracy, a secular state, Free Press, Free enterprise and human rights. Sunnis and Shias hate each other and try to destroy each other, but Sunnis and Shias are one in hatred of Israel and America. Just travel back in history for 1400 years. Then the truth will be clear.
Wherever Islam went, that place had been drastically changed, for the worse! There is a well-known, albeit, somewhat pluckish saying: “Islam can exist only in a desert, and if there is no desert, it will make one. “Look at Lebanon. Before 1970, Lebanon was the richest and most advanced

country in the Middle East. Lebanon, like USA and Western Europe, practiced tolerance and inclusiveness. It allowed Muslims to enter as refugees and helped them. Then after a few years, they started sectarian conflicts and ended up killing each other and the original denizens of the host country.

At present about 70 countries are involved in civil unrest because of Islamic terrorism. There are around 1.6 billion Muslims around the globe. Are they all terrorists or violent?

Of course not. According to some calculations only 25% are extremists. Still it is a large number constituting more than 400 million Muslims in the world. The majority of the Muslims are peaceful. When you look into history, most German people were peaceful, but Hitler changed all that and about 60 million people lost their lives. The fact that the majority are peaceful is irrelevant. It is also the case with Stalin's Russia and Mao's China. A brutal dictator or a psychopathic group of barbarians can change the world no matter how many are peace-loving and silent. The so-called "peaceful majority" is powerless and irrelevant.

Apologists for Islam say Islam means "peace" and the fundamentalist killers are a tiny minority. This canard has been repeated, either as a statement of appeasement or out of sheer ignorance, by some highly placed officials in American administration. One would hope that they know better. They have been contradicted, quite recently, by a well-known Islamic leader. He stated during a speech, "Islam is not a religion of peace, but a religion of submission." Polls conducted among Muslims offer some shocking revelations: 61% of Muslims worldwide believed that the Arabs did not carry out the attack on World Trade Centers on September

11, 2001; only 18% believed that they did. 77% of Muslims opposed the liberation of Afghanistan.

Islamic terrorists are like Africanized bees. Bees have been around for a long time. Living in harmony and having their place and function in the world, welcomed by everyone for their contributions and right to exist peacefully. The Africanized bee on the other hand, is tolerant of no other species or any non-Africanized bees. They will attack and kill everything else aggressively. All other species and any non-Africanized bee is their enemy. You can't de-Africanize a bee. You can only destroy it wherever you find its hive. Let us hope that we can wipe out the Africanized bees before they are the only bees left. It would be helpful if the regular bees understood this and separated themselves from the Africanized bees so that we could wipe out the bad bees and leave the good bees alone. Think about it bees. Our biggest obstacle is that we have an Africanized bee from "Hawaii" in charge of doing this job. And he refuses to use the word bee or Africanized.

Poll conducted among Egyptians in September 2002:

The majority (52%) of Egyptians supported the September 11 killings. Only 19% think Islamists did it, despite the fact the operation was led by an Egyptian! 39% thought Israel did it. The majority of Muslims in the world also supported suicide bombings and the destruction of Israel. Another interesting poll shows that almost all Muslims hate U.S.A. But another question was like this:

"In which country would you most like to live? Top answer is- U.S.A.

After 9/11, Palestinians danced in the streets to celebrate the killing of thousands of innocent civilians. The celebration took place also in many other Islamic Countries.
One of the most depressing aspects of the modern crisis has been how little soul searching there has been in Islam after 9/11.

An Indian Muslim, Muqtedar Khan, once said: "America is without a doubt one of the greatest countries in the world because it assumes we are moral beings and capable of doing good – we are free" He further stated "I know for sure that nowhere on earth including India, will I get the same sense of dignity and respect that I have received in the US." It is time that we acknowledge that the freedoms we enjoy in the U.S are more desirable to us than superficial solidarity with the Muslim world. If you disagree then prove it by packing your bags and going to whichever Muslim country, you identify with".

Thomas Friedman wrote in a December 3, 2008 article on the hypocrisy and silence of the Muslim world after the Mumbai terrorist attack asked, "After all, if 10 young Indians from a splinter wing of the Hindu Nationalist Bharatiya Janata Party travelled by boat to Pakistan, shot up two hotels in Karachi and the Central train station, killed at least 173 people and then, for good measure, murdered the Imam and his wife at a Saudi financed mosque while they were cradling their two year old son - purely because they were Sunni Muslims – where would we be today? The entire Muslim world would be aflame and in the streets"

As Ed Morrissey says: "Has Friedman seen massive protests in the streets against radical Islamist terrorists in these Muslim countries ever. Did any of them protest 9/11 attacks or the Madrid attack, Mumbai attack, London attack"?

Freedom of Religion

Many Muslims take personal offenses at any criticism of their religious beliefs. They find it very difficult to understand that "Freedom of religion" in the west means that people are free to criticize Islam as well as any other religion. This freedom is protected in the west. This is sometimes very hard for Arab Muslims to understand because they previously lived in Islamic countries, where any criticism of Mohammad or the Quran is viewed as a criminal offence punishable by death. Under Islam if you criticize Islam you die.

No religion, no matter how fervently believed or zealously practiced should be afraid of the searching light of scientific research. Since Muslims evidently have no problem whatsoever in openly criticizing other religions, why should they have a problem with those who for good and sufficient reasons criticize Islam.

After all, the same Bill of Rights that guarantees to Muslims the freedom to criticize other religions also gives other people the freedom to criticize Islam. The sword of religious freedom always cuts both ways.

Koran's tolerance of other religions

Koran 2: 191 "Slay unbelievers wherever you find them."

Koran 3:28 "Muslims must not take the infidels as friends".
Koran 3: 85 "Any religion other than Islam is not acceptable."
Koran 5:33 "Maim and crucify the infidels if they criticize Islam".
Koran 8:12 "Terrorize and behead those who believe in scriptures other than the Koran".
Koran 8:60 "Muslims must muster all weapons to terrorize the infidels."
Koran 8:65 "The unbelievers are stupid; urge the Muslims to fight them."
Koran 9:5 When opportunities arise kill the infidels wherever you catch them."
Koran 9:30 "The Jews and the Christians are perverts; fight them."
Koran 9:123 "Make war on the infidels living in your neighborhood."
Koran 22:19 "Punish the unbelievers with the garments of fire, hooked iron rods boiling water; melt their skin and bellies".
Koran 47:4 "Do not hanker for peace with the infidels; behead them when you catch them."

Wife Beating Sura 4:34

Men are in charge of women, because Allah hath made the one of them to excel the other, and because they spend of their property (for the support of women). So good women are the obedient, guarding in secret what Allah had guarded. As for those from whom ye fear rebellion, admonish them and banish them to beds apart, and scourge them. Translated by: Mohammed Marmaduke Pickthall.

"Islam is as dangerous in a man as rabies in a dog"
Winston Churchill.

Chapter 1

The Threat of Islam

It may sound ironic when I state that the greatest threat to peace in the world today is the "Religion of Peace," but irony becomes reality when we look at the widespread unrest created by the followers of that religion. More than any time since the crusade, Islam is posing a serious threat to the whole world. It now possesses the wealth and the weaponry to supplant the Soviet Union as the greatest threat to the world order created by the Judeo-Christian teaching on morality and ethics.

Islam is the fastest growing religion in the world today. Muslims now control about 50 of the world's most important countries from Indonesia in the east, through the oil rich states of the Middle East to Senegal on the Atlantic. At least 70 of the world's 190 countries are considered part of the Darul-Islam or House of Islam – land over which Islam rules. It is a religion practiced in the jungles of Africa, the sands of the Sahara, the oil fields of the Middle East, the mountains of Asia, and the islands of the Pacific. No Muslim true to his belief will deny that the Jews must die on Saturday, the Christians on Sunday and all other non-Muslims on any day of the week. The bottom line is that 1/6 of the world's population which is Muslim must convert or kill the other 5/6 of the world's population. Once that is accomplished, Muslims can turn on each other in a sectarian frenzy of killing. Sunnis believe that they are the only true Muslims; others are heretics and deserve to die. As far as this belief goes, there is hardly any difference between the original Islam of Arabia and the present day Islam of the world. From its inception, the motto has been the same: "Convert or Die". Muhammad practiced forced conversion. Those who resisted were beheaded or burned alive. Killing, raping, enslavement and other atrocities were practiced serially in the name of Islam for the last 1400 years, and the practice still continues among ISIS and Boko Haram and in small scale, among the tribal areas of Pakistan.

The Origin of Islam

Liberals and advocates of political correctness in the West think that they can reason with Islam through dialogue and negotiations. Left leaning liberals are always on the wrong side of history. They are naïve, delusional, and live in an imaginary world of their own. The best example comes from the Second World War. The following article would enlighten our knowledge about the Second World War.

John David Lewis, from the objective standard Vol.2, No.2

Author's note: This is the second of three articles for *The Objective Standard* dealing with military history and its (in this case implicit) lessons for modern day. The third article will consider the lessons of the American victory over Japan in World War II. These articles draw from my forthcoming book, ***Nothing Less than Victory: Military Offense and the Lessons of History from the Greco-Persian Wars to World War II*** (Princeton University Press).

"Imagine that an asteroid is heading toward the earth at thousands of miles per hour. While it is still far away, a small force can change its direction a few degrees and avert a catastrophic collision. But as it moves closer to the earth, the force needed to divert it multiplies exponentially, until only a massive explosion can prevent disaster. It would be one thing if men did not know of the asteroid, or saw it coming and were impotent to act. But suppose they had the bombs and the rockets needed to deflect it—but refused to do so because of "international opinion," a desire to spend the money on "social programs," or a claim that we must not interfere in the comet's own "natural" movements? This describes, in essence, Europe's drift into World War II.

During the 1930s, men stood at a cusp in time, a point of momentous decision, watching the growing power of Germany under its screaming, malevolent leader. Their failure to confront Germany—and the devastating consequences of that failure—demonstrate the power of ideas, both to motivate aggressors and to undercut defenders from taking the actions needed to protect freedom.

On September 1, 1939, twenty years and nine months after the armistice of November 11, 1918, that had ended

World War I, millions of Germans obeyed their Leader's call for a war of national aggrandizement and launched a new slaughter across Europe. The attack on Poland was the climax of five years of military buildup by Germany, which had followed fifteen years of feverish international diplomacy, economic transfers, and political agreements. Most European leaders had worked fervently to avoid a new carnage. They fell prostrate before Hitler's "Lightning War." The deepest reasons why so many Germans joined the armies of the Nazis, hailed their leader, followed their orders, and drank to their war cannot be found in reasons as shallow as economic stagnation, political dissatisfaction, or bad feelings about the last war. These factors were present in many nations that did not attack. In essence, the Germans were in the grip of a *philosophic pathology*, a set of ideas that told them it was morally good to sacrifice themselves and others to the all-powerful State, the Race, and the Leader. The power of these ideas in German culture was expressed in the mass support that the Nazis enjoyed among "Hitler's Willing Executioners."

But another force, outside of Germany, also pushed the world toward *blitzkrieg* and Auschwitz. This force too was a set of ideas—ideas in the minds of Germany's opponents—which prevented England and France from confronting Hitler when they could. In the mid-1930s, British politicians in particular were restrained from action, not by an *incapacity* to act, but by a lack of *will*. Certain moral ideals—which rose to the cultural forefront after the horrendous experience of World War I—conditioned British politicians and their constituents to become virtual allies of Germany in its drive to regain its status as a powerful nation. The result was a paralysis in the western European nations, which disarmed them as surely as any bomb and allowed Hitler to build up his forces to the point where his ability to fight exceeded that of his enemies.

The appeasement of Germany by Britain in the late 1930s has become a synonym for weakness, focused on a single man: Prime Minister Neville Chamberlain, who claimed "peace in our time" by handing over Czechoslovakia to Hitler in September 1938. But Chamberlain's appeasement, far from being a new, short-term plan by a weak man to deal with an emergency, was the culmination of a long policy that stretched back to World War I. The British desire for peace was conditioned by a set of moral ideas that hamstrung British leaders from recognizing the fundamental differences between their own nation and the German state, and the fundamental contradiction between the goals and policies promoted by leaders of the two nations. Those moral ideas gained cultural power in the aftermath of World War I. They sapped the will of the British people to oppose Germany when it was possible to do so, and left their leaders unable to take the steps needed to stop Germany from rearming. "

So notwithstanding the Leftist pipe dream, appeasement has worked rarely, especially, if the appeased have sinister motives like today's Islamic fundamentalists. As a matter of fact, all Muslims who pine for the so-called purity of the original Islam are at heart, fundamentalists biding for their time.

Muslims are the descendants of Ishmael. Ishmael was the son of Abraham and his Egyptian wife, Hagar. Genesis 16:11-12 records the angel of the Lord as saying to Hagar, "You are now with child and you will have a son. You shall name him Ishmael. He will be a wild donkey of a man;

his hand will be against everyone and everyone's hand against him, and he will live in hostility toward all his brothers."

Abraham was 75 and Sarah, his wife, 65, when God entered into covenants outlined in Genesis chapter 12. When Abraham turned 86 (11 years after the promise), Abraham stumbled in his faith and tried to help God fulfill the promise about the son. He applied the old saying "God helps those who help themselves." But that is not a verse in the Bible. The fulfillment of the promise of a child at age 75 came after 25 years: (Genesis 21:5).

Some decisions we make in life carry consequences far beyond our comprehension. They are something we would give anything to undo, but alas, they cannot be. What is worse is the fact that there are some sins that are generational; that is, the consequences of our wrong choices can extend to our relatives for generations. Abraham had a lapse of faith concerning God's promise to give him a son. The decision he had made during this period of unbelief resulted in enormous consequences that have continued through centuries until this very hour.

It is interesting to note the character of Hagar in Genesis 16:3-4. "So after Abraham had been living in Canaan ten years, Sarai his wife took her Egyptian maidservant, Hagar, and gave her to her husband to be his wife. So he went in to Hagar, and she conceived. And when she (Hagar) knew that she was pregnant, she began to despise her (Sarai)." Here, Hagar's attitude was ungrateful, prideful, selfish and arrogant.

The seeds of enmity are expressed in embryonic form on the occasion of Isaac's weaning in Genesis 21:8-11. "Isaac grew and was weaned. And Abraham made a great feast on the day that Isaac was weaned. And Sarah saw the son of Hagar the Egyptian, which she had borne unto Abraham, making sport. Wherefore she said unto Abraham, 'cast out this bondwoman and her son; for the son of this bondwoman shall not be heir with my son, even with Isaac.' And the matter was very displeasing in Abraham's sight on account of his son." This is the last we hear of Ishmael until the death of Abraham and the coming together of Isaac and Ishmael to bury Abraham in Hebron alongside Sarah. (Gen. 25: 7-11)

Now to understand a frequently ignored verse in the Old Testament: "And Sarah saw the son of Hagar the Egyptian making sport." The Hebrew word "metzahek" has a number of meanings, all of which are, to use the expression, "off color." The King James Edition of the Bible tries to sanitize sexual aspects of the Hebrew Bible and uses the expression "And Sarah saw Ishmael behaving in a haughty manner." (Gen. 21:8-14) But is it logical to assume that Abraham, the patriarch would expel his beloved first-born son Ishmael for being "haughty"? Whoever believes he or she has never been haughty is very naughty!

Clearly then, the King James provides a politically correct mistranslation. The word "metzahek" has sexual connotations. True, the word "metzahek" also means "mocking", but still, is that a reason for Abraham to expel his first-born beloved son Ishmael? Although Ishmael was a wild donkey, don't we love our own children even if they are on the wild side? Very often, wild children are even more beloved because they need love. There had to be something much worse. Later in chapter 26 verses 8-9 state that, "It came to pass, when he (Isaac) had been there a long time, that Abimelech King of the Philistines looked out of a window, and saw, and behold, Isaac was 'sporting' (metzahek) with Rebecca his wife. And Abimelech called Isaac, and said, "Behold, of a surety she is thy wife; and how did you say, 'She is my sister'?" So the correct meaning of what Sarah saw: Ishmael, sodomizing or sexually molesting her son, Isaac. One must not forget that Ishmael was about 16-17 years old with his little brother being 3-4 years old.

Ishmael wanted to show his male superiority over Isaac and his preeminence in inheriting Abraham rather than the little challenger, Isaac. Ishmael wanted to show his dominance. It is a commonly known practice in Islamic Middle East for homosexual acts to be carried out against weaker males to show just who the boss is. September 11, 2012: Islamists took over the US consulate in Benghazi, Libya and sodomized and killed Ambassador Christopher Stevens.

Ishmael, the father of the Muslim people, was not only a wild donkey, but a sexual pervert as well. In the Islamic Paradise, girls as well as boys are available for Muslims. This is the reason Abraham expelled him from his house.

Genesis 26:34, "When Esau was forty years old, he took as wives Judith, the daughter of Beeri the Hittite, and Basemath, the daughter of Elon the Hittite. And they were a grief of mind to Isaac and Rebekah." When Esau, the older son, marries two women leaving the curse of Ham and Canaan that are hateful in the eyes of God and his parents, it would seem that this sets the stage for the younger son to get the blessing. In Genesis 27:40 a blessing is given to Esau, "By your sword you shall live." In Genesis 28:9, finally we see the curse placed on Esau by his father, Isaac, "You will live by the sword." After marrying two Canaanite women, Esau then goes off to marry the daughter of Ishmael (Mahalath). He then goes on to become an Ishmaelite living with his uncle. Esau and Ishmael are to be considered one, unit. Ishmael was a sexual pervert, a wild donkey, in constant warfare with his brethren, according to Genesis 16:12. And Esau's blessing from Isaac which was really a curse, was "You shall live by the sword" (Genesis 27:40). Thus, the characters are the same.

Hebrews 12:15-16, "Looking carefully lest anyone fall short of the grace of God; lest any root of bitterness springing up cause trouble, and by this many become defiled; lest there be any fornicator or profane person like Esau, who for one morsel of food, sold his birthright." Ishmael and Esau did become one unit. They represent one idea, the sword and constant warfare. They represent Islam. Today, the Judeo-Christian Western world and democracy are under attack by Esau-Ishmael Islamic barbarism and totalitarianism with a different god: Allah, the moon god, war god and sword god; the Koran, the antithesis of the Bible, and their Mahdi, who is returning a second time to kill Jews on Saturday and Christians on Sunday.

It is startling that the Arabic language has almost a thousand names and synonyms for sword. It is important to note today how many Arab countries have the insignia of the sword in their national logos.

Islamic Invasion of America: The 20 Point Plan
July 1, 2009 Report: The Muslim Brotherhood Project in America

On November 7, 2001, international law enforcement authorities and Western intelligence agencies discovered a twenty-year-old document revealing a top-secret plan developed by the oldest Islamist organization with one of the most extensive terror networks in the world, to launch a program of "culture invasion" and eventual conquest of the West. This document is known as "The Project." Will America continue to sleep through this invasion as they did when we were attacked on September 11, 2001?

1. Terminate America's freedom of speech by replacing it with statewide and nationwide hate – crime bills.
2. Wage war of words using black leaders like Louis Farrakhan, Rev. Jesse Jackson and other visible religious personalities who promote Islam as the religion of African-Americans while insisting Christianity is for whites only. What they fail to tell African Americans is that it was Arab Muslims who captured them and sold them as slaves. In fact, the Arabic word for black and slave is the same, "Abed."
3. Engage the American public in dialogues, discussions, and debates in colleges, universities, public libraries, radio, TV, churches and mosques on the virtues of Islam. Proclaim how it is historically another religion like Judaism and Christianity with the same monotheistic faith.
4. Nominate Muslim sympathizers to political office to bring about favorable legislation toward Islam.

5. Take control of as much of Hollywood, the press, TV, radio, and the internet as possible by buying the related corporations or a controlling stock.
6. Yield to the fear of imminent shut off of the life blood of America – oil. (Fortunately, in the last few years, America has found more oil at North Dakota's Bakkan Field and Texas Eagle ford. Now America is the top oil producer in the world.)
7. Yell foul, out of context, personal interpretation, hate crime, Zionist, un-American, inaccurate interpretation of the Koran any time Islam is criticized or the Koran is analyzed in the public arena.
8. Encourage Muslims to penetrate the White House, specifically with Islamists who can articulate a marvelous and peaceful picture of Islam. Acquire government positions and get membership in local school boards. Train Muslims as medical doctors to dominate the medical field, and research and pharmaceutical companies. Take over the computer industry.
9. Accelerate Islamic demographic growth via:
   a.) massive immigration (100,000 annually since 1961)
   b.) Use no birth control whatsoever; every baby of Muslim parents is automatically a Muslim and cannot choose another religion later

   c.) Muslim men must marry American women and Islamize them (10,000 annually), then divorce them and remarry every five years – since one can't legally marry four at one time in USA. This is a legal solution in America.
   d.) Convert angry, alienated black inmates and turn them

into militants (so far 2,000 released inmates have joined al-Qaida worldwide). Only a few "sleeper cells" have been captured in Afghanistan and on American soil.

10. Reading, writing, arithmetic and research through the American educational system, mosques and student centers (now more than 2500) should be sprinkled with dislike of Jews, evangelical Christians and democracy. There are currently more than 300 exclusively Muslim schools in the U.S. which teach loyalty to the Koran, not the U.S. constitution. In January of 2002, Saudi Arabian Embassy in Washington mailed 4500 packets of the Koran and videos promoting Islam to America's high schools. If you visit Saudi Arabia and you carry a Bible, Saudi customs will throw that Bible in the trash.
11. Provide very sizeable monetary Muslim grants to colleges and universities in America to establish "centers for Islamic studies" with Muslim directors to promote Islam in higher educational institutions.
12. Let the entire world know through propaganda speeches, seminars, local and national media that terrorists have hijacked Islam, when in truth, Islam hijacked the terrorists.
13. Appeal to the sensitive Americans for sympathy and tolerance towards Muslims in America who are portrayed as mainly immigrants from oppressed countries.
14. Nullify America's sense of security by manipulating the intelligence community with misinformation.
15. Form riots and demonstrations in prison system demanding Islamic Sharia as the way of life, not America's justice system.

16. Open numerous charities throughout the U.S., but use the funds to support Islamic terrorism with American dollars.
17. Raise interest in Islam on America's campuses by insisting freshmen take at least one course on Islam.
18. Unify the numerous Muslim lobbies in Washington, mosques, Islamic student centers, educational organizations, etc.
19. Send intimidating messages and messengers to the outspoken individuals who are critical of Islam and seek to eliminate them by hook or crook.
20. Applaud Muslims as loyal citizens of the U.S. by spotlighting their voting record as the highest percentage of all minority and ethnic group in America.

Abuja Declaration Goals and Strategies

This organization was founded on 28 November 1989 in Abuja, Nigeria with the goal to win the whole of Africa to Islam. The statutes and goals were ratified in 1991, and marked her formal definitive founding.

A battle plan was composed to Islamize Africa with some less innocent points in that decision:

a. To ensure only Muslims are elected to all political posts of member nations.
b. To eradicate in all its forms and ramifications all non-Muslim religions in member nations (such religions shall include Christianity, Ahmadiyya and other tribal modes of worship unacceptable to Muslim). The word Christianity is underline in the declaration.

c. To ensure the ultimate replacement of all western forms of legal and judicial systems with the Sharia in all member nations.
d. To ensure the appointment of only Muslims into strategic national and international posts of member nations.

The execution of this strategy can be recognized in countries like Nigeria, Ethiopia and Sudan.

Population Bomb

Around 70 percent of global population growth over the next 30 years will be in Muslim countries as the Muslim population of 1.6 billion is growing at twice the rate of the global population, thus representing the fastest growing consumer segment in the world.

Britain and the rest of the European Union are ignoring a demographic time bomb: a recent rush into Europe by migrants, including millions of Muslims, will change the continent beyond recognition over the next two decades, and almost no policy-makers are talking about it.

The numbers are startling. Only 3.2 percent of Spain's population was foreign-born in 1998. In 2007, it was 13.4 percent. Europe's Muslim population has more than doubled in the past 30 years and it will double again in 2015. Europe's low white birth rate, coupled with faster multiplying migrants, will change fundamentally the European culture and society.

Britain's Muslim demographic is now so dominant that the British government recently began to allow Islamic civil and religious law, known as Sharia, to be enforced alongside British law. But if religious tolerance is good, why is this a problem? This is not an issue of religious liberty. Islam is not designed to co-exist with western civilization; it is designed to conquer it.

There are presently 85 Sharia courts all across Britain. Honor-killing represents a new and growing form of homicide in many European countries, whereby Muslim families collaborate to kill fellow family members, in order to restore honor. This practice is not alien to the U.S. In 2009, a Muslim man beheaded his wife, confessed to authorities, and still received a scheduled award from the Council of American Islamic Relations (CAIR).

In 2005, France experienced massive Muslim riots in 300 cities. Public buildings were fire bombed, 200 policemen were injured, and 4000 were arrested. This is not unusual as a Muslim response to perceived offenses. Remember the Danish cartoons and the consequences. (Please Google search to find out more information.)

The central problem is assimilation. Most Muslims don't want to be British or French. Muslims come for the wealth of the West, and to make the West Muslim. The evidence is transparent to anyone paying attention. The Paris riots of 2005 were committed by second and third generation children of Muslim immigrants. The ultimate aspiration of Muslims is total, global domination within the theocracy known as a "caliphate." Be they peaceful Muslims or radical Muslims, all share this goal.

The problem of Muslim integration is so sensitive that 751 areas have been willingly ceded to Islamic residents by the French government. Called "no-go zones" by many, these areas are off-limits to non-Muslims who value their lives. The UK is home to an indistinguishable number of "no-go zones", with violence toward non-Muslims increasing in once-peaceful areas. Dutch Muslims have such a grip on Holland that those who speak out, must live in safe houses like Dutch parliamentarian Geert Wilders. Many areas of Germany are now off limits to police and other uniformed personnel, as in France and the UK.

Islam sanctions deception to achieve their goal. The deceptive treaty is known as the Hudna Agreement, which states: Negotiate peace with your enemy until you become strong enough to annihilate him. This is the justification chairman Yasser Arafat gave to his critics who condemned him for signing the Oslo agreement. Allah is known in Arabic as "Al-Macker" or the cunning one, or the greatest of all the liars and deceivers.

On October 30, 2013, the London stock exchange launched the Islamic market index. The index will help Islamic investors comply with Islamic principles around finance. Prime Minister David Cameron announced that Britain will be the first country outside of the Muslim world to issue its own Islamic bond, known as "Sukuk."

Invasion of Europe by Muslim Refugees

The refugees started to come to Europe after the Middle east was destabilized by Arab spring uprising. The refugee influx reached its climax in 2015. Almost five million Muslims have arrived in Europe as refugees. ISIS has claimed that they have infiltrated the refugee population. The European leaders especially the German leadership are in a suicidal path by accepting all the refugees without any documentation.

Czech President Milos Zeman has called the current wave of refugees to Europe "an organized invasion", adding young men from Syria and Iraq should instead "take up arms" against the Islamic State of Iraq and the Levant (Isil) group.

"I am profoundly convinced that we are facing an organized invasion and not a spontaneous movement of refugees," said Zeman in his Christmas message to the Czech Republic released on Saturday.

He went on to say that compassion was "possible" for refugees who are old or sick and for children, but not for young men who in his view should be back home fighting against jihadists.

"A large majority of the illegal migrants are young men in good health, and single. I wonder why these men are not taking up arms to go fight for the freedom of their countries against the Islamic State," said Zeman, who was elected Czech president in early 2013.

Massive rape my Muslim men in Europe on New Year's Eve in December 31.2015

Breibart News. London

by Oliver Lane 4 Jan 2016

Just five arrests have been made by German police after central Cologne was transformed into a war-zone on New Year's Eve, as an estimated 1,000 migrants celebrated by

launching fireworks into crowds and sexually assaulting German women caught up in the chaos.

The sordid details of the horrifying sexual assaults and attacks made against ordinary Germans by large gangs of migrants in Cologne in the early hours of Friday morning are just now emerging.

Far from a small number of sex assaults reported to have been made by German speaking men in initial reports on New Year's Day, dozens of women are now reported to have been molested and "raped", while dozens more men have been assaulted and robbed.

One victim, 28-year-old 'Katja L' spoke of her ordeal as she tried to make her way to the waiting room of Cologne railway station with two other girls and a boyfriend in the early hours of new year's day. She said to *Der Express* – one of the largest regional newspapers: "When we came out of the station, we were very surprised by the group that met us there". She said the group was "exclusively young foreign men". Keeping close to her friends, they pressed on:

"We then walked through this group of men. There was an alley through [the men] which we walked through. Suddenly I felt a hand on my buttocks, then on my breasts, in the end, I was groped everywhere. It was a nightmare. Although we shouted and beat them, the guys did not stop. I was desperate and think I was touched around 100 times in the 200 meters.

"Fortunately I wore a jacket and trousers. a skirt would probably have been torn away from me".

As Katja L and other witnesses who have since come forward said, as they were molested by the gang the men were laughing and pulling their hair, and there were shouts of (Rape, Rape ") hurled at them as they were called "sluts". Treating her as "fair game", there had been so many men groping at her Katja L said she would be unable to positively identify any of the perpetrators to the police.

Others were less lucky. One woman had her tights and underwear torn off by the crowd, and a police source quoted "there had been "rapes" at the station that night.

So far, police have identified 80 victims of the gangs, 35 of which were subjected to sex attacks. Others were assaulted or robbed. Officers suspect there are many more as of yet unreported cases from the night, and are appealing for victims to come forward after their ordeals."

A press conference hosted by Cologne's chief of police Wolfgang Albers this afternoon confirmed the attacks had been perpetrated by migrants, all of whom were found to be carrying official immigration paperwork by police officers at the time. Mr. Albers said "the crimes have been committed by a group of people who mostly come from her in appearance from the North African and Arab countries", and that he found the situation "intolerable".

In addition to the sex attacks, there were several brawls between migrant gangs at the railway station, and large numbers of fireworks were fired into the crowds and at the hapless police. A witness said: "There were thousands of men. Simply firing into the crowd, and as my girlfriend and I wanted to get us to safety, but they blocked our way. We were so scared! We fled from the station".

Why rape by Muslim men are universal throughout history.?. Muslims believe that If you are not a Muslim, you have no value. If a Muslim rape or kill a non-Muslim, Allah will be pleased in them. The life of a non Muslim is worthless without Allah. So death for a non-Muslim is a blessing for the victim. Muslims are putting them out of their miserable life without Allah. Many people say that terrorists are not true Muslims and Islam is a religion of peace. But the definition for peace is different for a Muslim. When all the infidels are eliminated Islam would establish peace on earth. Actually ISIS represents true Islam. Moderate Muslims do not follow Koran and Hadith closely.

Chapter 2

A World Gone Stupid

Islam is an enemy that is bound and determined to defeat the United States and rid the world of both Christians and Jews - the very enemy that has planted 150 pro-terror Muslim Student Associations in the top 150 universities and colleges across the nation, that are paid to carry out their activities by funds from student unions. Yet the leaders of the Muslim student Associations are never questioned, even though evidence of their support for terror is demonstrable and extensive.

Since the Oslo Accord, the PLO terrorists have the seal of approval from the White House. They enjoy visits from top terrorist chain and funding to the tune of hundreds of millions of dollars.

They even receive training from the" United States." War on Terror" – The PLO is no different from Hamas. Westerners love to bank on Muslims who do not agree with

Osama Bin Laden, but what these Western experts fail to realize is that for many of these so called "moderate" Muslims, their only disagreement with Osama is his timing. Westerners do not understand that when it comes to the Muslim world, even the most moderate of Muslims –if they are religious - all believe in the coming of Mahdi and the establishment of the caliphate to rule the entire Globe by changing world laws to adopt the Islamic Sharia. The coming of the Mahdi to religious Muslims is as holy a belief as the coming of Messiah is to Christians and Jews.

To many Muslims, Osama had simply acted in haste and did not gain the proper permission from officially sanctioned Islamic Jurisprudence. According to orthodox Islamic Jurisprudence, only a sitting caliph has the authority to declare a global Jihad. Thus to many Muslims, Osama jumped the gun.

Think about it- someone acted too soon is very different from thinking that what someone did was actually evil. Westerners are gullible and they believe half statements of the Muslims as true. For example, if we say to a Muslim that we hate Hitler, the Muslims also will say that "Sure we hate Hitler too" But when the Muslims are alone they would say among themselves," we hate Hitler because he never got the job done" Thus half statement can be totally misleading.

Research into the early history of Islam reveals that Jews who refused to convert were slaughtered by the founders themselves - Mohammad, Omar his disciple, Ali his nephew, and the rest of the caliphs. Muslims all over the world always follow the example of Mohammed. When one questions a supposed moderate Muslim, it is always important to ask the right questions: Did Mohammed massacre the Jews of Arabia? Yes, or No?

In 1976, the Muslim World League issued a fatwa that declared that belief in a coming Mahdi is universal for all Muslims. While tradition varies between Sunni and Shia regarding Mahdi's appearance on the world stage, the core belief in his coming is not a sectarian issue but is accepted by the majority of Muslims worldwide. Although there is some difference in the beliefs of these two major sects the essence of the belief in the Mahdi is the same.

Mahdi

Mahdi for Sunni Muslims was "The rightly-guided and awaited one". Shia Muslims refer to him as "Sahib AL – Zaman" - The Lord of the Age" This is exactly what the Bible calls Satan "The Lord of the Age" (2 Cor. 4:4)

Khilafa

According to Islamic tradition, the Mahdi doesn't merely merge as some vague religious leader. He will return to reinstate the office of the Caliphate. Islam directs its followers: "If you see him, go and give him your allegiance, even if you have to crawl over ice because he is the vice-regent (Khalifa) of Allah, the Mahdi.

Hadith

The Hadith or Sunna is the record of both the words and deeds of the prophet Muhammed. In other words, the Quran is "thus says Allah" and the Hadiths are "thus says Mohammed". The Hadiths are crucial to understand when one debates with Muslim apologists. Whenever a non - Muslim brings up the issue of Islamic terrorism, the standard Muslim person will ask" show me a single verse in the Quran that teaches violence." This has been a common technique used to throw off westerners with whatever verse is given; it will then be explained away as speaking of self-defense or as commandments that were only given on one particular occasion. In other words, all of the commandments in the Quran that call Muslims to Jihad are obsolete and not applicable today.

But this is sheer trickery. If a Muslim denies the authority of the Hadith, then he is denying Mohammed's authority as a prophet. Quran says "O you who believe, obey God and obey his messenger and those in authority among you (Quran 4:59). Some wiggly Muslims will deny Hadith in front of you to save face. This is comparable to a Christian denying the New Testament.

For true Muslim theologians the quality of revelation in Quran and Hadith is the same; only the mode of expression is different. Hadith is the Quran in action. In the Quran, Allah speaks through Muhammad; in the Sunah, Muhammad acts through him... Thus Muhammad's life is a visible expression of Allah's sayings in the Quran. Muhammad is a living example of the Quran. Quran and Hadith provide equal guidance for every situation in life, such as Muhammad's dress, diet, toilet manners, hairstyle sexual and other habits. Islam controls all aspects of a Muslim from birth to death. When Islam conquered other parts of the world, Muslims destroyed local languages and replaced them with the Arabic, and replaced existing local culture with Islamic culture.

Muslims usually give Muhammad's name for the male child and try to mimic his behavioral pattern.

Few westerners realize that Muslims are allowed to conceal the truth regarding this issue when they are speaking to non-Muslims. Sunna explains and provides details for the laws found in the Quran. There are no serious scholars today who would deny the 200 or so commandments found in the Hadith, which promote nothing short of jihad by the sword including unprovoked invasion for the sole purpose of advancing Islam.

Always keep in mind, the difference between Islam and Christianity. It can be summed up in one statement- Christianity is Calvary, Islam is Cavalry. Allah commands all of these followers to engage in Jihad until there is literally no one left on earth who does not worship Allah".

Caliph

Historically the Caliph is the supreme political, military and administrative leader of all Muslims worldwide. The Caliph is the Vicar of Mohammed as the Pope is the Vicar of Christ to Catholics worldwide. The office and government of the Caliph is known as the Caliphate (Khilafat). It is the only form of government that is fully sanctioned by Islamic jurisprudence.

But since 1924, after nearly fourteen centuries of "divine rule" the office of the Caliph was finally abolished. With the mandate to have both seats of the Mahdi and Caliph as one, Mohammed said," There would be a Caliph in the last period of my ummah- He would be Imam Mahdi. In other words, this last Khalifa, when he is installed, would be the Mahdi of the End Times.

The Muslim Jesus

The second most important Muslim end-time character is Isa-al Maseeh, the Muslim Jesus. The Jesus of Islam is in no way a "Savior" or "Redeemer". He is merely one more prophet out of a long line of prophets sent by Allah. The special title of Messiah, although retained in the Islamic tradition, actually is void of any truly Biblical Messianic qualities. In Islam, Jesus will come back as a radical Muslim to lead the Muslim armies to abolish Christianity and to slaughter the Jews.

The Antichrist and Mahdi

Most western Christians understand the Anti-Christ to be only an imposter-one who claims to be Jesus Christ, though he is not. This view lacks the deeper nuance that the Bible ascribes to the Antichrist. On the one hand the Antichrist attributes to himself titles that belong to Jesus alone, but on the other hand, he also bears several titles that exhibit his clear opposition to Christ and all that he stands for. The "Antichrist refers to the fact that he will be both against Christ and all that Christ stands for, while at the same time, he will also attempt to be a replacement for Christ. The Antichrist will be Anti-Trinity, Anti Son, Anti crucifixion and Anti-God –in- the flesh.

Islam's theology fulfills these denials perfectly; every Muslim in the world denies all of these doctrines. Better than any other religion, Islam is a perfectly tailored Polemical response which stands firmly against the most crucial aspects of the nature of God as described in the Bible.

Allah and Satan are called the Deceiver. When anyone picks up the Bible, he is almost immediately confronted with the fact that Satan is the greatest deceiver in history. It was shortly after having eaten the forbidden fruit that Eve said "The serpent" (Satan) deceived me, and I ate "(Gen 3:13) In the New Testament, John the Apostle reminded us all that anyone who denies that Jesus has come in the flesh" is the deceiver and the Antichrist "(2 John 1:7)

Paul the apostle elaborated on the deceptive role of the Antichrist when he also warned of the coming of the lawless one who will be in accordance with the work of Satan displayed in all kinds of counterfeit miracles, signs and wonders and in every sort of evil that deceives those who are perishing (2 Thess:2:9-10). And as the Bible concludes, it encourages us all with the fact that in the end "the devil, who deceived them (will be) thrown in to the lake of burning sulphur" (Rev 20:10)

Allah brags by calling himself Khayrul -Makireen, which literally means the Greatest of all Deceivers (Quran 3:54). He refers to Himself with such a title in Quran 8:30;27,50;13,42;10,21; (14,46) ;(43,79;86,15,6; 7,100).

But what are the circumstances in Quran 3:54 that are causing Allah to be deceptive? Interestingly the deception is regarding the story of Jesus, as verse 55 states "when Allah said to Jesus, I shall cause you to die, then will raise you up to myself" ...Allah deceived the people by not allowing Jesus to die on the cross and resurrecting Him instead.

As Christ was going about doing His Father's work, Satan was concocting schemes for his firstborn Mohammed. All of the most revered interpreters of the Quran; 1bn Katheer, Al-Tabari, Al-Jalalyn and Al-Qurtubi interpret Quran 3:54 as referring to Allah deceiving people to believe that Jesus was crucified when he was not. Qurtubi observes that some scholars have considered the words "the best of schemers" to be one of God's beautiful names. Thus, one would pray, "O Best of schemers, scheme for me"! Qurtubi also reports that the prophet used to pray, O God, scheme for me and do not scheme against me".

How is it that in the Bible it is the devil and his vessel the Antichrist that are respectably referred to as the schemers, liars and the deceivers but in the Quran, it is Allah who is the greatest of all deceivers? Satan knows fully well who he is and as he was inspiring the Quran, he couldn't help but brag a little. The Arabic word "Makara" means to deceive, scheme, hatch up, cook up or connive. The Arabic Bible in Genesis 3:1 uses the same word for Satan.

In Ahl-Al quran (International Quranic center) Sharif Sadeq explains the meaning of makara as attributed in the Quran: "conniving is a weapon, like any other weapon, could be used for good or evil like a knife or a gun". According to Sharif, there are two types of conniving, one which is forbidden and the other which is noble.

Both attempt to Deceive Christians and Jews

Not only do Satan and Allah share the characteristics of being deceivers par, excellence, they also both love to specifically target one group above any others- Ahlul-Kitab or "The people of the Book (the Bible)" as the Quran calls them. The Bible warns that Jews and Christians are Satan's favorite targets, yet in the Quran and all throughout this "sacred" text, they are targeted by Allah.

Does not Jesus warn, "For false Christ and false prophets will appear and perform great signs and miracles to deceive even the elect –if that were possible (Matt 24:24??) The Quran, like the book of Mormons lack historic evidences.

The Quran borrowed some apocryphal verses and old folk tales. Where is the Quranic Archaeological Review? What happened to the "Book of Mormon Archaeological review? Have there been any Nephites and Lamanites found? The same goes for the Muslims.

Why would the Muslim authorities put such a tight lid on the volumes of the oldest Quran found in Al-Masjid, Al-Kabeer in Yemen? However, If you wish to purchase a facsimile copy of the codex Vaticanus, you can do so.

Why are copies of the Top Kapi manuscript, considered one of the oldest Quranic manuscripts, still sitting unexamined in the Top Kapi museum in Turkey? What are they afraid of? Why can't the oldest Quranic manuscripts face the same kind of critical examination that the most ancient Biblical manuscripts have endured for centuries?

The Dead Sea scrolls were found to validate the authenticity of the Bible. In Quranic style, typical Muslim challenge, bring your proof if you are truthful.
Who is lying- Christians or Muslims?

The Biblical Picture of the Last Days is one where deception is the absolute rule of the day in virtually every passage where the end –times are discussed.

In the New Testament, these authors stress that believers are to be very careful that they are not to be deceived. (Matt 24:3-4)
Likewise, the apostle Paul warned this in (2 Thess. 2:9-12).

Most westerners have a hard time relating to the fact that purposeful exaggerations covering the truth and outright deliberate lying are actually part and parcel of the religion of Islam. Now, of course, if you bring this matter up to a Muslim, he will be quick to quote the Quran (II: 42) which says: "Do not mix the truth with the falsehood, nor hide the truth while you know it."

But unfortunately if we dig just a little deeper to examine the meaning of this "thou should not lie" command and turn to the ancient Quranic commentary (Tafsir) by Ibn Katheer, we find a very different explanation. Allah forbade the Jews from intentionally distorting the truth with falsehood and from hiding the truth and spreading falsehood and mixing the truth with falsehood, nor concealing the truth while you know the truth. So Allah forbade them (the Jews) two things: He ordered them to make the truth known, as well as explaining it- Qatadah said that "And mix not truth with falsehood means: "Do not mix Judaism and Christianity with Islam while you know the truth that the religion of Allah is Islam and that Judaism and Christianity are (corrupted) innovations that did not come from Allah. The very verse that Muslims point to in an attempt to claim that they are forbidden from lying means nothing of the sort, but is, instead, a command to Jews not to lie to Muslims.

This is only the tip of the iceberg with which the western Titanic is colliding. What lies beneath the surface and is hidden from view is far more ominous? While evangelism in Christianity is "Good News that Jesus Christ died for you," Islamic evangelism is violence with a shout of "Islam is Victorious" and "Allah is great. "For whom is this good news! You must make a choice between Allah and the blade; you need to understand how the victims of Islam get set up. It begins with the famous saying of Mohammed "War is deception".

Many Muslims will even lie for monetary gain when they deal with non-Muslims. The fallacy that guides them is: The end justifies the means, even with conspiracy to murder.

Imam Al-Ghazali, one of the most famous Muslim theologians of all time, encourages lying as long as any positive or beneficial goal may be achieved. Remember the Ten Commandments "Thou shall not lie," Ghazali also instructs Muslims to lie in order to attain material prosperity.

Even many so-called moderate Muslims, in order to protect the image of Islam as the Religion of peace, lead double lives. Most westerners swallow much of the Islamic deception, hook, line and sinker.

Who are the Palestinian People?

In A.D. 70 the Romans destroyed the Jewish temple, deported people and minted a coin to celebrate their achievement. The coin bore the inscription "Judea Capta". The Roman emperor was Titus. Another Jewish revolt took place in A.D. 113. The third revolt took place in A.D. 132. The Jews held out until A.D. 135. Emperor Hadrian proclaimed Jerusalem and all of greater Judea out of bounds to all Jews, and as a final act of spite; he renamed the country Palestine after the Jews' hereditary foe, the Philistines. This is the way that the name "Palestine" entered Latin, Church history and literature. Neither a Palestinian state nor a Palestinian people have ever existed in history.

Chapter 3

Misguided Western Media and Leftists

Today the western world is living in a politically correct but morally corrupt society. Political correctness is eroding the foundation of western nations. Even Israel has embraced secularism and political correctness. Many modern historians in Israel are rewriting history and paint Orde Wingate in negative terms. Orde Wingate was the founder of the Israeli army.

Modern pacifists behave like the Sanyasi (Hindu Priest) who did not want to hurt a fire ant that got onto his beard. So he went to the den of the fire ant and placed his long beard so that the solitary fire ant on his beard might get out. But what happened was just the opposite. A thousand new ones got onto his beard and bit him.

Ronald Reagan the greatest President after Washington and Lincoln understood the importance of confronting evil. 'Trust but verify" he warned, describing the perils of dealing with evil communists and other ten horn dictators. Those who refuse to see evil for what it is are doomed to relive history's tragic lessons. •History always repeats itself and prudent visionaries shall avoid the repetitions of evil and errors.

The Holocaust

This generation has been secure from tyranny and oppression. We tend to undervalue the sacrifices of our predecessors. Many leftists have a hard time recognizing evil abroad because of their disdain for American values. The self-loathing leftists promise socialism. They never dared to live a few months in Asia and Africa. These multimillionaires and billionaires have their own planes and many mansions, and they hate America's prosperity and goodness. Their attitude is that America doesn't deserve its prosperity, and that we are unfairly exploiting a disproportionate share of the world's resources. They always talk against corporations. But there are no corporations in Cuba and Zimbabwe. These foolish leftists are not aware of the fact that they are living longer with a better quality of life from the medicines that were invented by evil corporations. Who invented medicines to treat such maladies as diabetes, cholesterol, high blood pressure, cancer, and other life-threatening diseases? Liberals have no problem using smart phones, computers, GPS, and cars made by corporations.

The 1930's world saw the birth of fascism and Nazism - two pillars of evil that are linked with the cruelties of the Stone Age. Nazism was rooted in Socialism, totalitarianism, virulent anti-Semitism, and hatred of Biblical Judeo-Christianity.

Useful Idiots

In political jargon, the term "useful idiot" was used to describe soviet sympathizers in western countries and the alleged attitude of the soviet government towards them. Those sympathizers were naive, foolish, or in willful denial, and were being cynically used by the Soviet Union. The term had been coined by Vladimir Lenin to describe those western reporters and travelers who would endorse the Soviet Union and its policies. Lenin totally despised them in his heart.

Today, even after evidence of massive man-made famines in the communist world, after Solzhenitsyn's revelations about the Gulags and after the horrors of the killing fields of Cambodia, the useful idiots continue to deny or downplay staggering human tragedies under communist dictatorships. Socialist dictators have slaughtered more people in the twentieth century than all other centuries combined. Mao Tse-tung of China, Joseph Stalin of Russia and Polpot of Cambodia stand out among other socialist murderers.

Amil Imani has succinctly described the characteristics of Islam's useful Idiots. "Islam enjoys a large and influential ally among the non-Muslims: A new generation of "useful idiots," the sort of people Lenin identified living in liberal democracies that furthered the work of communism. This new generation of useful idiots also live in liberal democracies, but serve the cause of Islamo fascism -another virulent form of totalitarian ideology.

Useful Idiots are naïve, foolish, ignorant of facts, unrealistically idealistic, dreamers, willfully in denial or deceptive. They hail from the ranks of the chronically unhappy, the anarchists, the aspiring revolutionaries, the neurotics who are at war with life, the disaffected, alienated from government corporations and just about any and all institutions of society. The useful Idiot can be a billionaire, a movie star, an academe of renowned politician or from any other segment of the population. The useful idiot derives satisfaction from being anti- establishment. He finds perverse gratification in aiding the forces that aim to dismantle an existing order, whatever it maybe: an order he neither approves of nor he feels he belongs to. Most of them have been married multiple times, and are very unhappy. Their wealth cannot buy peace and happiness. So they blame Christians and conservatives. Ronald Reagan was right when he declared that "Liberalism is a mental disorder."

The useful idiot Is conflicted and dishonest. He fails to look inside himself and discover the causes of his own problems and unhappiness which he readily enlists as causes that validate his distorted perception. Understandably, it is easier to blame others and the outside world than to examine oneself with an eye of self-discovery and self-improvement. Furthermore, criticizing and complaining – liberal practices of the useful idiot - require little talent and energy. The useful idiot is a great armchair philosopher and 'Monday morning quarterback"

The useful idiot takes things much farther. The useful idiot, among other things is a master practitioner of scapegoating. He assigns blame to others while absolving himself of responsibility. He has a long handy list of candidates for blaming anything and everything on and by living a distorted life, he contributes to the ills of society.

The useful idiot may even engage in willful misinformation and deception when it suits him. Terms such as "Political Islam" or "Radical Islam" for instance are contributions of the useful idiot. These terms do not even exist in the native parlance of Islam, simply because they are redundant. Islam, by its very nature and according to its charter - the Quran– is a radical political movement. It is the useful idiot who sanitizes Islam and misguides the populace by saying that the "real Islam" constitutes the main body of the religion, and that this main body is non-political and moderate.

Regrettably a large segment of the population goes along with these nonsensical euphemisms depicting Islam because it prefers to believe them. It is less threatening to believe that only a hijacked small segment of Islam is radical or politically driven and that the main body of Islam is indeed moderate and non-political. But Islam is political to the core. In Islam the mosque and State are one and the same- the mosque is the state. This arrangement goes back to the days of Muhammad himself. Islam is also radical in the extreme. Even the 'moderate' Islam is radical in its beliefs as well as its deeds. Muslims believe that all non -Muslims, are going to hell and well deserve being maltreated compared to believers. They are comfortable to commit most heinous barbaric atrocities. So for a strict Muslim rape and murder is sanctioned by their faith.

Muslims are radical even in their intra- faith dealings.

Various sects and sub- sects pronounce other sects and sub-sects as heretics' worthy of death. Women are treated as chattel, deprived of many rights; hands are chopped for stealing even a loaf of bread; sexual violation is punished by stoning and much more. These are standard day to day ways of the mainstream moderate Muslims living under the Stone Age laws of sharia. By the way bestiality is very common in Islamic countries.

The 'moderate' mainstream of Islam has been outright genocidal from its inception. Their own historians record that Ali, the first Imam of the Shia and the son in-law of Muhammad, with the help of another man beheaded 700 Jewish men in the presence of the prophet himself. The prophet of Allah and his disciples took the murdered men's women and children in slavery. Muslims have been and continue to be the foremost practitioners of slavery.

The slave trade, even today, is a thriving business in some Islamic lands where wealthy, perverted sheikhs purchase children of the poor from traffickers for their sadistic gratification. Muslims are taught deception and lying in the Quran itself- something that Muhammad practiced during his life whenever he found it expedient. Successive Islamic rulers and leaders have done the same. Khomeini, the founder of the 1979 Iranian Revolution, for instance, rallied the people under the banner of democracy. All along, his support for democracy was not a commitment of an honest man but a ruse. As soon as he gathered the reins of power, Khomeini went after the useful Idiots of his time with vengeance. The best children of Iran having been thoroughly deceived and used by the populist-religionism had to flee the country to avoid the fate of tens of thousands who were imprisoned or executed, raped and killed just as men are slaughtered without due process or mercy. Most of the liberals are Kool-Aid drinkers similar to most people in the Middle East. They will believe any story without authentication. Khomeini ordered all boys between 12 and 18 to go and fight Saddam Hussain. They were given a few days of training and each boy was given a golden colored key to open the door in paradise. The keys were made in China. Most boys perished in the Iraqi border when they stepped on the mine field of Saddam Hussain.

The lesson is clear. Beware of the useful idiots who live in liberal democracies. Knowingly or unknowingly they serve as the greatest volunteer and effective soldiers of Islam. They pave the way for the advancement of Islam and they will assuredly be among the very first victims of Islam as soon as it assumes power.

Amil Imani is an Iranian-born American citizen and pro-democratic activist. (Most of the above article on useful idiot was taken from Amil Imani's essay)

If Islam takes over the west, do you know, who they would behead first: The homosexuals, abortionists and pornographers, and Hollywood liberals who are the purveyors of these evils. So Sean Penn, Rosie O' Donnell, Michael Moore and all other useful idiots will be beheaded first. The liberals do not want to live in a Socialist "workers' paradise" of Asia, Africa or Latin America. Those who fail to learn history and recognize evil are doomed to fall into the trap of appeasement.

Terrorism, despotism, and liberalism are equally evil. The lessons of history are clear: You cannot negotiate with evil. You can't sweet-talk it. You can't compromise with it.

You cannot give ground to it like Ariel Sharon gave the Gaza strip to Hamas to stop sending Rockets to Israel. Instead of bringing peace, The Hamas are killing innocent civilians by sending rockets. You can only destroy evil.

Liberals want to find out why Muslims and others hate America; Liberals blame America for the pollution of the planet and the destruction of the ozone layer. According to the Looney left, Americans are responsible for all human suffering and oppression. And no matter how far America bends over backward to accommodate, liberals accuse and still blame America for discrimination and injustice.

Why did the hijackers attack America? Because they were evil to the core, they were hateful and jealous and destructive. Muslims have created nothing for the past seven hundred years and their only contribution to world history has been death, oppression, slavery, conversion, fear and terror. Liberals want to understand our enemies. They bought books on Islam. They think we might have provoked them to attack. In the words of Michael Savage "A liberal is someone who wants to understand the guy who just broke into this house, who burned the place down, who raped his wife and who murdered his kids. Yes, the liberal wants to discover what he or she might have done wrong to deserve the attack."

The conservative doesn't care what religious affiliation the civilian hides behind, what holy robes he may wear or what he calls himself. When he sees the enemy coming to rape his wife and kill his children, the conservative shoots him dead before he gets in the house. He doesn't shake his hands and get a book out to study the belief system of the murderer.

In 1776, Thomas Paine said "what we obtain too cheap, we esteem too lightly; it is dearness only that gives everything its value". The problem with a liberal is that you've been handed everything on a silver platter, the truth is, you do not know how good you've got it in America. This may help: **There is only one country in the world that attracts people from virtually every other country". Why? America is the magnet for seven billion people. Christian faith with personal freedom and Capitalism made America the magnet of the World**. Conservatives see things much different than liberals. America is a superior society not because Americans are superior human beings, because American culture was founded on recognition of our God given natural rights –the "unalienable rights" referred to in the declaration of Independence. From that awareness flow a basic, shared respect for humanity, individual liberty, limited government, and the rule of law.

Ronald Reagan used to remind his Soviet counterparts, we have the power to conquer any nation but we don't. "We have the power to enslave any people but we don't. We have the power to loot any nation of its natural resources but we don't. Instead, America sends her young men and women to war to defend the weak; she sends her resources to help the poor all over the world without any reservation." Liberals preach the value of peace and against all wars. Yet many of America's greatest moments have come when its people have taken up arms to defend liberty. Was it war mongering when America defeated the Axis powers of Hitler, Mussolini and Japan and liberated millions in World War II? Ronald Reagan defeated communism and liberated more than a billion people from communist atrocities. America also liberated 26 million people of Afghanistan and 25 million people in Iraq.

Know your Friend and Foe

If you know your enemy, you can fight him effectively. America's inability to understand the enemy became evident in the days immediately following September 11, 2001. Our Leaders called the terrorists "cowards" The reasoning is that the terrorist targeted women and children. But the fact is that the terrorists did not care who was on the hijacked planes or in the World Trade Center. Their targets were the symbols of American capitalism and of the American government. Like Japanese kamikazes, the terrorists were certainly fanatical, but they were not cowards.

A second enduring myth about terrorists is that they were poor and miserable. They carried out these terrible acts because they were desperate or more likely insane. Several commentators argued that the terrorists are drawn from the "wretched of the earth" In this view, "they strike out against the affluent West because they have nothing to live for.

But these theories do not square with the facts. Lunacy theory can be tested by releasing a bunch of insane people from asylums. Could they have pulled off what the terrorists did? Of course not. The truth is that the terrorists were educated people who knew how to fly a plane. In 2007, Great Britain foiled the terrorist attack by arresting home grown Muslim doctors. Most of the terrorists came from rich families. Osama Bin laden was a multimillionaire. It is foolhardy and irrational to dismiss the Islamo fascists this way.

What motivates Islamo fascists? One vital clue is the diary composed by Muhammad Atta and circulated to the other terrorists prior to the attack. "Out of respect to Allah, it says, cleanse your body, shave off excess hair, wear cologne and tighten your shoes. Read the Quran and pray through the night in order to purify your soul from all unclean things. Try and detach yourself form this world because the time for play is over. Keep a steadfast mind because anything that happens to you could never be avoided, and what did not happen to you could never happen to you. On the morning of the attack, pray the Morning Prayer and do not leave your apartment unless you have performed ablution. Pray as you enter the plane and recite verses from the Quran. Ask God to forgive your sins and to give you the victory. Clench your teeth as you prepare for the attack. Shout "Allah Hu Akbar". Strike your enemy above the neck as the Quran instructs. Moreover "if you slaughter, do not cause discomfort to those you are killing, because this is one of the practices of the prophet, peace be upon him" Finally **"you should feel complete tranquility because the time between you and your marriage in heaven is very short" New York Times,29September 2001, B-3.**

These are not the instruction of cowards or lunatics, but of deeply religious Muslims. It is a mistake to regard them as "suicides" in the traditional sense. A suicidal person is one who does not want to live. These men wanted to live, but they were prepared to give their lives for something they deemed higher. They ultimately wanted to live in Paradise with 72 virgins. It is difficult for those of us who live in a largely secular society to understand that people would willingly, even happily give their lives for their faith.

When a few people show such tendencies, we deem them extremists, when large numbers of people do, we convince ourselves that they have been brainwashed. They believe they are martyrs but we pronounce they are not really Muslims. President Bush even suggested that they were betraying their faith. British Prime Minister Tony Blair has said he regrets to the term "Islamic terrorists" because the vast majority of Muslims are not terrorists. (John O'Sullivan)

The reason for such waffling is that USA and its allies know that terrorism and anti-Americanism have substantial support among the whole Islamic World.

Muslims in the West try to give a soft meaning to the word Jihad" **They say that Jihad is an internal struggle in the soul against sin**. They misinterpret this word to avoid shame and embarrassment to their religion.

But the Quran itself urges Muslims to "slay the idolaters wherever you find them and lie in Ambush everywhere for them" The Quran, Trans N.J. Dawood Page 186. In his classic work, the Muqaddimah, the influential Muslim writer Ibn Khaldun asserts "In the Muslim community, holy war is a religious duty, because of the obligation to convert everybody to Islam whether by persuasion or by force" Ibn Khaldun, the Muqaddimah (Princeton university Press: Page 183). These passages convey how Muslims themselves have usually understood their religious mission. Historian Bernard Lewis writes that the traditional Islamic view, upheld by the vast majority of Jurists and commentators is that Jihad usually refers to an armed struggle against infidels and apostates.
Lewis writes:

"In the Muslim world view, the basic division of mankind is into the House of Islam (Dar-al-Islam) and the House of war (Dar-Al-Harb). Ideally the House of Islam is conceived as a single community. The logic of Islamic law, however, does not recognize the permanent existence of any other polity outside Islam. In time, in the Muslim view, all mankind will accept Islam or submit to Islamic Rule. A treaty of peace between the Muslim state and a non-Muslim state was, thus in theory, impossible. Such a truce, according to jurists, could only be provisional. The Muslim terrorists are operating squarely within the Islamic theory. Indeed, they are performing what Islam has typically held to be a religious duty. Daniel Deleanu succinctly quoted from Islamic writings **"If one permits an infidel to continue in his role as a corrupter of the earth, the infidel's moral suffering will be all the worse. If one kills the infidel, and this stops him from perpetrating his misdeeds, his death will be a blessing to him".**

Islam makes it incumbent on all adult males, provided they are not disabled or incapacitated, to prepare themselves for the conquest of other countries so that the law of Islam is obeyed in every country in the world. Those who know nothing of Islam pretend that Islam counsels against war.

When Bin Laden invokes the name of Salah-al-Din (Saladin), he is drawing inspiration from the great twelfth-century Muslim general who threw back the crusaders and recaptured Jerusalem. In his videotaped statement released on Al Jazeera television, Bin laden said Americans should get used to suffering because "our Islamic nation has been tasting the same for more than 80 years. "He was referring to the dismembering of the Ottoman Empire, the last of great Muslim empires, by the victorious European forces after World War 1.

Some people argue vehemently that Islamo fascism does not exist. But there is something horribly familiar about today's Islamist movement. Like the fascism of Hitler and Mussolini, Islamism is based on a cult of murderous violence that exalts death and destruction and despises the life of the mind. Both are bitterly nostalgic for past empires and lost glories and bent on avenging various historical humiliations at the hands of "inherently inferior" outsiders. The Islamists, like the Nazis have a particular loathing for Jews, homosexuals and women. And for Islamists, as for fascists, the ultimate goal is to establish a vast, unconquerable territory- a "Caliphate" as the jihadists call it, where their power and ideology will reign unchallenged. All over the world, thousands are dead and maimed because Muslim killers believe they can attack civilians at will and the West is too weak to stop them. Many are oblivious of their intentions. And behind their physical attack on America and the West is an intellectual attack, one that we should understand and be prepared to answer.

Chapter 4

The Threat of Islam: A critical study

Mosques Replacing Churches in the West

Today, in many cities in England, there are more Muslims than Christians and there are more mosques than churches. "Funded by the vast resources of Arab oil money, the Muslims are buying abandoned churches and turning them into mosques at such a rate that some Muslims claim that England will soon be the first Muslim European country." (Robert Morey) Today there are more than 1500 mosques existing in Great Britain. Islam is also growing rapidly in Australia, Canada, Germany and the United States.

Threat of Islam

Contrary to the old Cold War, we can be hit by a major attack and not know exactly where to retaliate. The best example is the three coordinated and simultaneous attack in Bombay, India in July 2011. It killed and maimed many. The government is helpless to find out and eliminate these people. The enemy hides in the shadows and mingles with citizens of a targeted country. In America, these terrorists are protected by America's doctrine of "political correctness," which has hamstrung our intelligence agencies and rendered them uncatchable.

They have targeted the following places:

1) Our major bridges, such as the Golden Gate or Oakland Bay Bridge.
2) Tunnels entering New York City.
3) Railways, shopping malls and sports stadiums
4) Banks and Stock Exchange etc.

In the 21st century, it is hard to imagine how a 4000-year-old family feud could cause the whole world to become involved. Yet this is exactly what the Bible predicted would happen in the last days. The prophecies spelled out an exact scenario of events that will come together shortly before the end of history as we know it. Central to this scenario is the re-igniting of the ancient conflict between the Israelites and Arabs. The conflict has risen and subsided at various times since the destruction and dispersion of Israel in 70 A.D.

It is as a consequence of the rebirth of the state of Israel that the Bible prophets predict the whole world will become involved. The Bible predicts what will be the final flashpoint that ignites the war of Armageddon. It will be an unsolvable dispute over Jerusalem between the sons of Isaac and Jacob and the sons of Ishmael and Esau. We know these people today as the Israelis and the Arabs. Who can believe that a small, backward, neglected land that had become so desolate would become the focal point of the world? For centuries, world attention focused on the Gentile Civilizations of Europe, America, Russia and Far East. Until the middle of the 20th century, many people couldn't even find Palestine on a map. But today, the headliners aren't about Western or Asian civilizations; they are about the people of the Middle East. For the first time in modern history, ancient Bible names are making global headlines. Today the world's focus has returned to a place that had been bypassed by the modern developments of science and technology.

Emperor Napoleon Bonaparte, while on his Palestinian campaign, asked one of his generals,
"Can you give me proof that the Bible is the Word of God?" He replied, "Your Majesty, the Jew, against all historical precedence, has survived centuries of dispersion and yet has remained a distinct people – a nation in exile – though scattered over the entire world and terribly persecuted, just as the Hebrew prophets predicted he would be, patiently waiting for his promised return to the land of his fathers." Napoleon Bonaparte, 1798.

The Root Cause

It is impossible to understand the present Middle East crisis without knowledge of exactly what happened then, and why. This all began at a time when all nations were determined to push the knowledge of the one true God out of their culture and memory. The Bible records that because of this, God chose a man for the purpose of creating a special nation. God's purpose for this nation was to preserve a true revelation about Himself, to reach out to the world through it and ultimately to provide salvation for all mankind. God chose Abraham and made a covenant with him.

God promised a son through whom a nation would be created. God anticipated anti-Semitism and gave the promise of Divine Protection. "I will bless those who bless you, and I will curse him who curses you." Abraham and his divinely chosen line of descendants through Isaac and Jacob have been consistently persecuted. There is a mystical quality behind the intensity of hatred toward Israel. This is especially true of the descendants of the southern kingdom that is composed of the tribes of Judah, Benjamin and Levi. They were first called "Jews" while in Babylonian captivity. The name "Jew" was derived from the name of their geographical origin, Judea. The Jews have been singled out for special hatred since they were driven into global exile after the destruction of Israel in 70 A.D. The name "Jew" has come to be indiscriminately applied to survivors of all the twelve tribes of Israelites in recent centuries.

The Origin of Anti-Semitism

There are false teachers within the church today who would deny that the Israelites have a right to the land of their forefathers. They are known by such titles as Dominionists, Preterits, Amillennialists, or Post-millennia lists. What is common to all of these theological systems is that they allegorize all unfulfilled Bible prophecies and covenants, especially those that apply to the future of Israel. They say that the covenants were "conditional," and therefore were cancelled by Israel's rejection of Jesus Christ as Messiah. They teach that Israel has no future in God's plan as a distinct people and nation; they teach that the church inherited all of these covenants and promises when Israel rejected their Messiah, Jesus the Christ.

In other words, they believe that the church has now become "Israel" in place of the natural descendants to whom the promises were exclusively made. This is called "Replacement Theology." Augustine laid the ground work for this teaching in the fifth century A.D. He taught that the church had become Israel and was now God's kingdom on earth. This became the rationale for the "conquistadors" to conquer and pillage the Americas in the name of the Roman Catholic Church. It also was the philosophy that set up the "Holy Roman Empire" over Europe. This resulted in such shameful atrocities as the Crusades and the inquisitions "in the name of Jesus." The actions violated the most basic teachings of Jesus Christ. The knights of Europe, under the orders of the Popes, slaughtered tens of thousands of innocent people, particularly the Jews.

In the first century Roman Church, some Christians were inclined to turn against the Jews and think they had permanently replaced them in God's plan. The answers are given by Paul in Romans 11:25-29. (Isaiah 59:2 and Romans 9:27-28; Isaiah 10:22-23)

The apostle Paul reveals that God's present rejection of Israel is not total, nor is it final. It is temporary until the full number of Gentiles is saved. Then he quotes specific promises of God that guarantee that "all Israel will be saved when the Deliverer (the Messiah) comes from Zion in the second coming."

The practice of allegorizing these specific promises, which started with the fifth century theologian Augustine, became the foundation of anti-Semitism in the church. Sadly, anti-Semitism spread from the Church to the rest of the world. If the curses are literal, the promises are too.

Predictions of the Final Restorations

The following predictions cut to the heart of the current Arab-Israeli conflict. They show that the title deed to the land of Israel was never revoked. It is still binding on the basis of the Divine oath by which it was originally given. Moses, at the end of the message, made the predictions of their ultimate restoration. Deut.30:1-5. **1** "So it shall be when all of these things have come upon you, the blessing and the curse which I have set before you, and you [1]call *them* to mind [b]in all nations where the Lord your God has banished you,

2 and you return to the Lord your God and [1]obey Him with all your heart and soul according to all that I command you today, you and your sons,

3 then the Lord your God will restore [1]you from captivity, and have compassion on you, and will gather you again from all the peoples where the Lord your God has scattered you.

4 "If your outcasts are at the ends of the [1]earth, from there the Lord your God will gather you, and from there He will [2]bring you back.

5 "The Lord your God will bring you into the land which your fathers possessed, and you shall possess it; and He will prosper you and multiply you more than your fathers."

It is important to note that God does not say "if," but "when" throughout His prediction. This is because God views the repentance as certain, since He will cause it to happen. It is also very clear that God addresses this promise to the believing remnant of the physical descendants of Abraham, Isaac and Jacob – not to some allegorical offspring in the Church. Ezekiel also speaks of this final restoration from the worldwide Roman dispersion: Ezekiel. 16:59-63.

However, God anticipated that Israel would despise His oath and break the Mosaic covenant. He warns that He will discipline them, as they deserve. Yet, despite all they will do, He promises that He will fulfill to them the covenant made with their fathers. The traditional prophetic view of many mainline churches that are based on unwarranted allegorical interpretations of these passages has caused great chaos and suffering to the descendants of Abraham, Isaac, and Jacob.

Ezekiel predicted Israel's final restoration to the land and rebirth as a nation in the "Last Days." It is imperative to note the sequence of this prophecy. [Ezekiel. 36:22-28]

Ezekiel's Outline

Ezekiel lays out more clearly than any other prophet the sequence of events in the Last Days. Ezekiel 36 emphasized the miracle of the land's restoration when God returns His people to it. The prophecy focuses on the desolate condition of the land that the surrounding nations (which are all Muslim today) have brought upon it. God warns of terrible judgment upon these Muslim nations who have "taken His Land."

Ezekiel 37 emphasizes the miracle of returning the dispersed Israelites from all the nations where they have been scattered for centuries. He interprets the scattered bones as the whole house of Israel. He reveals that the open graves are the nations, where the people have been scattered. The miracle of Israel's national rebirth is illustrated by all of the bones coming out of the graves and joining together.

Ezekiel 38 reveals the momentous event of history that will finally bring the Israelites to fruition in their true

Messiah. The prophet Zechariah foresaw this climactic event over 2500 years ago. Zech. 12:10, 13:1.

Through the centuries until this very hour, the consequences have effected about a hundred generations over a period of 4,000 years.

God predicted that the Ishmaelites would live to the east of all his brethren. God gave them the Arabian Peninsula, which is to the east of all the rest of Abraham's descendants. The migrant Arab is called a "Bedouin." He loves the desert and the freedom to move about the vast barren regions from oasis to oasis, always searching after every green thing. His hand will be against everyone and everyone's hand will be against Him.

This characteristic has been dominant throughout the history of the Arabs. Blood feuds have been fought between the many Arab tribes for centuries. If an Arab is forced out of the protection of his tribe, he usually doesn't last very long. The wild donkey reflects this very characteristic. He groups together in small herds and is hostile with even other herds of his own kind. Similarly, Arab society, from its earliest history, divided up into many clans. Only two things united them: Mohammad and hatred for the Jews.

Enmity Flashes in Embryonic Form

The seeds of enmity are expressed in embryonic form on the occasion of Isaac's weaning. Genesis 21:9 gives the incident. When Ishmael scoffed at and made fun of Isaac, he did so with the knowledge that according to Divine Revelation, Isaac was the chosen one." Unbelief, envy, and pride of carnal superiority were the causes of Ishmael's conduct. God's promise to Israel – Genesis 17:20-21.

God Hears Ishmael

The meaning of Ishmael is God Hears. Genesis 21:17-19 – Ishmael's Legacy.

Ishmael had twelve sons, each of whom became a great prince and founded a nation. However, the second son, Kedar, became the most powerful and wealthy. His descendants figure prominently in Arab history. God blessed Ishmael and caused him to live 137 years. (Genesis 25:17-18)

Never in history has there been a family feud that sustained such enmity over so long a period of time. And no other ethnic violence has ever affected so many nations as this one is about to do. Indeed, the Bible predicts that the last war of the world will be triggered by a conflict between the descendants of these ancient family members.

This is why it is pivotal to trace these peoples through history to the present day. And it is of ultimate importance to understand the root cause of the common hatred they have all embraced toward Israel. Western diplomats and media have no clue about the root cause of these issues.

Abraham's nephew Lot, also cursed his sons, and they became enemies of Israel. They are Moab and Ammon.

Abraham's Other Sons

When Sara died, Abraham was 137 years old. After Abraham chose Rebekah as a wife for Isaac, making sure the covenant line was settled, he married another wife. He was about 139 by this time. Abraham married Keturah. (Genesis 25:1-4)

Abraham had six more sons and ten grandsons before his death at the age of 175 years. These are the people the prophet Jeremiah refers to in a prophetic warning to the nations that mistreated Israel. He refers to them as a part of the Arabian people. (Jeremiah 25:24) The mixed multitude is the descendant of Abraham's other sons, who mingled with the Ishmaelites in the vast Arabian Peninsula.

Before Abraham died, he gave all he had to Isaac (Genesis 25:6). Abraham gave gifts to the sons of the concubines, and while he was still alive, he sent them outward, away from Isaac his son, to the country of the east. The country to the east was the land that became known as the Arabian Peninsula. There was resentment and jealousy among the sons toward Isaac. They saw only the father's favoritism, not God's sovereign purpose. This is the common factor that runs through all of Israel's relatives. It is this enmity that developed from envy and jealousy which bind all of these family members together.

"Esau I Have Hated"

There are two descendants of Abraham that have been the most persistent enemies of Israel: Ishmael and Esau. Esau was nicknamed "Edom" or Red, apparently for two reasons. First, because, from birth, his body was covered with red hair; and. Second, because he called the lentil stew for which he sold his birthright, "that red stuff."

Genesis 27:35-40 describes the blessings of Isaac to Esau. Like his uncle Ishmael, Esau would live by the sword.

Throughout the history of Israel, the Edomites took every opportunity to vent their hatred against them. When Israel came out of captivity from Egypt, the Edomites would not even let them pass through their land. [Numbers 20:21] God graciously spared Edom, despite the fact this brought great hardship upon Israel.

God Warns Amalek

Amalek, one of the Edomites chiefs, was a persistent enemy of Israel. (Exodus 17:14-16)

Edom Becomes a Larger Symbol

Ezekiel foretold that God would judge all Edom (referring to all Arabs) for appropriating Israel's land. (Ezekiel 36:5) Also (Amos 1:11-12). Psalm 83 prophetically tells us of the final mad attempt by the ancient descendants of Abraham's other sons to destroy Israel. It shows that Edom and Ishmael are linked together and leading the conspiracy to wipe Israel off the earth.

Edom and Ishmaelites are primarily Arab people. The descendants of Moab, the Hagrites, Gebal, Ammon, Amalek and Philistia melted into the mixed group that were absorbed by the Arab culture and later converted to Islam. Today, these people make up the nations of Jordan, Saudi Arabia, UAE, Oman and Tyre, which is now Lebanon. Assyria is Syria; and Persia is Iran. All of these people are linked together by their common continuous enmity toward Israel.

The Origin of Islam

From the beginning, Islam's spread was accomplished through physical violence, bloodshed, and war. The violence was not only against non-Muslim infidels, but also against fellow Muslims. Mohammed taught and practiced violence from the beginning. The Bible gives the genealogy of Ishmael to demonstrate that God kept His promise to him: Genesis 25:12-18

The second son, Kedar, is the most frequently mentioned son of Ishmael. He became the most powerful and wealthy of all his brothers. Ezekiel mentions them in Chapter 27:21. This is part of a prophecy about Tyre's destruction, which was fulfilled by Alexander the Great. We also find some of the descendants of Abraham's sons through Keturah. They are mentioned in the same prophecy as being part of the Arab peoples. (Ezekiel 27:20, 22)

Isaiah predicts that the wealth of Nebaioth (Ishmael's first born) and Kedar will be offered to the Lord at His second coming when He sets up His kingdom in Israel. [Isaiah 60:7]

Chapter 5

Quran's Interpretation of History

According to Islamic teaching, Abraham (Ibrahim) did not stay in Canaan with Isaac, nor send his other seven half-brothers to the land of the East. Muslims teach that Abraham went to Mecca where he raised all eight sons together. They also believe it was Ishmael, not Isaac, whom Abraham offered as a sacrifice on Mount Moriah before the angel stopped him. They believe that Ishmael was the chosen one of God, not Isaac. This is the basis of their denial of the Biblical covenants that are specifically confirmed to Abraham, through his line of descendants from Isaac, Jacob and his twelve sons. It is on this basis that Muslims claim all the land of Israel and Jerusalem.

The Arab's Warring Nature

The writer of Psalm 120 gives insight into the violent nature of the descendants of Kedar. (Psalm 120:5-7) Both secular and Biblical sources describe the Arabs, especially the sons of Kedar, as a people who continuously fought. (Isaiah 21:13-18) The sons of Kedar were especially known for being expert archers. Kedar's father, Ishmael, was an archer. (Genesis 21:20)

The Extent of Arab Territory

The descendants of Kedar were wealthy and powerful merchants, known as the Nabateans. They ruled the region as Arabia Petra. Petra, the capitol, was a famous banking city built into a natural fortress in the mountains of Edom. During the Greco-Roman times, this kingdom covered the northern part of the Arabian Peninsula.

Petra was known as the "Lost City" until archeologists rediscovered it in the 19th century A.D. The way it was constructed made it one of the wonders of the ancient world. The Ishmaelites captured most of the Middle East. The Ishmaelites absorbed other peoples, such as the descendants of Esau/Edom and other sons of Abraham from Keturah. The Ishmaelites are Arabs.

Arabian Society and Government

The Arabians began as nomadic tribes, or clans, in the deserts. They were known as Bedouins. Clan organization is the basis of the Arab Bedouin Society. There is one supreme chief over the clan and he is called the Sheik. The clan is composed of many families. A family unit dwelt in one tent. Violence is endemic to Arabian culture. Violence has been a continual fact of life for the Arabs. This is a common thread that runs throughout historical accounts of their culture.

Gen 26:39-40 “Your dwelling will be away from the earth’s richness, away from the dew of heaven above. You will live by the sword. The Edomites first lived in the mountains of Seir, but over the centuries many were forced to flee to the desert of Arabia where there is little “richness of the earth or dew from heaven “They have always lived by the sword.

The Arabian Religion

Long before the founding of Islam, the Arabs lost faith in the one true God whom their forefathers Ishmael, Esau and the sons of Keturah knew. They degenerated into polytheism and worshipped holy rocks and trees. These objects were not deemed sacred because they were indwelt by the spirits called “Jinns” (later known as “genie”) Arabs believed (and noted in the Quran and Hadith) that “jinns” were a category of spirits halfway between angels and men. They believed that they could be good or bad, though most are considered to be malicious. They can possess animals and inanimate things such as rocks, trees, wells etc.: Jinns were adopted into Muslim theology and Quran. Arab lore was replete with legends of jinns. With the coming of Islam, Mecca had the distinction of being the most important religious center. It was a major oasis on the main caravan route from earliest times. Mecca developed first because it was the site of the sacred Zamzam well, which Arabs believe that God revealed to Abraham and Ishmael.

The Kabah

The Quraysh tribe made sure that there was an idol for every religion at the pagan temple called the Kabah. The word Kabah is Arabic for “Cube “and refers to the square stone temple in Mecca where the idols were worshipped. At least 360 gods were represented at the Kabah and a new one could be added if some stranger came into town and wanted to worship his own god in addition to the ones that were already represented. Muhammad destroyed idols belonging to other tribes, but spared the figurines of Jesus and Mary, and adopted Allah as god of everyone. Allah was Muhammad's own tribal god. In pre Islamic days, there were not only intense trade contacts between Indian and Arab pagans, but also a kind of pilgrimage exchange. **The Hindus visiting Arabia paid their respects to the Arab sanctuaries and considered the black stone in the Kabah as "Shiva Lingam", the phallus of Siva. The Arabs in there turn, went to pray at the Somanath Temple in Gujarat. Muslims believed that the idols of the pagan goddesses Al-Lat and Manat (mentioned in Rushdie's ("Satanic Verses") had been transferred to Somanath. This is one reason why Muhammad Ghaznavi and other Muslims risked their lives in conducting raids deep into Hindu territory in order to destroy the Somanath Temple**. ("Nagationism in India" by Koenraad Elst. Page 117.)

Mecca's greatest significance came from being the site of the special religious altar known as the Kabah. It is a 50-foot cubic structure of gray stone and marble, positioned so that its corners correspond with the four points of the compass. The Kabah contained 360 idols- one for each of the lunar calendar days. The cornerstone of the Kabah was the sacred Blackstone. It is a meteorite of very ancient origin. It was and is believed to have the power to absorb sin from the one who kisses it. Arabs believe that the Blackstone is a god who protects their tribes.

The Hierarchy of Gods

In the Arab Pantheon of gods, five were most important in their hierarchy. They were Uzza, Allat, Manat, and Hubal. The first three were female, which formed a tritheistic relationship. On the other hand, Hubal was a male moon deity. He was believed to have originated in Babylon.

It is Hubal that is represented in the Hilal, Islam's symbol of the crescent moon. The star is believed to represent Uzza, the morning star goddess. Hubal was also believed to be the guardian of the Kabah.

The fifth and highest of all deities was called "Allah". He was worshipped as the supreme creator as well as the "father" of the tritheistic female goddesses.

The Mecca Pilgrimage

Mecca, with the Kabah, the sacred Zamzam well and the presence of the highest deities became the religious vortex of the Arabian Peninsula. Arabs from all over the land began to come on pilgrimages to Mecca, long before Mohammad. It was because of the lucrative business brought by the pilgrims, that possessing the guardianship of the sacred Kabah and Zamzam well became a prize to be sought.

Rivalry for Holy Sites.

From approximately 100 BC the Kabah and its sacred well were under the control of the tribe known as the Beni Jurham. In about the third century A.D, they seem to have been driven out and replaced by an Ishmaelite tribe known as the Khuzaa.

Then in about A.D 235, Fihr, the leader of another Ishmaelite tribe, the Quraysh, married the daughter of the Khuzaa tribal chief. Later, in about A.D 420 Qusai, a descendant of Fihr married the daughter of another Khuzaa Chief of Mecca. Although he was not of the Khuzaa tribe, Qusai made himself virtually indispensable to his father-in-law, who was the guardian of the Kabah. As a result, Qusai was given the custodianship of the coveted sacred key of the Kabah.

When the khuzaa died, Qusai claimed custody of the Kabah for the Quraysh. One of his first acts was to relegate the Khuzaa clan to a subordinate position. Qusai ordered the building of a semi-permanent housing around the Kabah. He also shrewdly restructured the tribal social order. He instituted tribal council meetings and a hall was built near the Kabah for this purpose.

The Quraysh Tribal Religion

It was not coincidental that the Quraysh Tribe from which Muhammad's family came was addicted to the cult of the moon god, Allah. They witnessed the pilgrims coming to Mecca every year to worship circling the Kabah seven times, kissing the Blackstone (considered their special tribal talisman that guaranteed their Protection and blessing) and then running down to the nearby Wadi to throw stones at the devil. Mohammad was destined to grow up with these religious traditions. So it cannot be an accident that all of these religious traditions are prominent in the Muslim religion, which he supposedly received by original, divine revelation.

The rivalries continued throughout the centuries. The Quraysh tribe prevailed as guardians of Mecca's holy sites by the sixth century AD. Within the Quraysh tribe, a man named Hashim married a woman named Selma, who gave birth to a son, Abdul-Al-Mut-Talib.
Abdul had seven sons- Harith, Talib, Lahab, Jahal, Abbas, Hamza and Abdullah.

Abdullah married Amina, who was a descendant of Qusai's brother Zuhra. Abdullah's wife, Amina gave birth to a son whom they named Mohammad. With this event, the entire history of the Arab people was about to take a paradigm shift.

Muhammad is a conundrum of history. Apart from the acceptance that a supernatural being worked in and through him, there is no way to comprehend him. This one man is solely responsible for the Arabs exploding out of the Arabian Peninsula, and in less than 100 years, conquering lands from the Atlantic to the borders of China, from North Africa to Spain and into the gates of Vienna in Europe. If the Muslim hordes had not been stopped by the Frankish King, Charles Martel, also known as "Charles the Hammer "at the Battle of Tours in AD 732, all of Europe would have fallen under Islam's control.

The life and times of Mohammad

Muhammad was born around AD 570 and died in July of AD 632. His father was from the Quraysh tribe. This tribe gained much power and influence, both for their commercial activity in Mecca, and because they were the guardians of the sacred well and the Kabah with its black meteorite cornerstone. They enjoyed prestige, influence and profit because of the continuous religious pilgrimages all Arabia made to Mecca's "holy sites". The Quraysh was devoted to Allah, the Moon god, and especially to Allah's three daughters who were viewed as intercessors between the people and Allah.

Muhammad's father was Abd -Allah, or Abdullah who was reputed to have been quite handsome. Marriages were strategically calculated for political and economic goals and Abd Al Muttalib was seeking an alliance with the Banu Zuhra (Shura) clan. Thus he arranged for Amina Bint Wahib to marry his son Abdullah. Muhammad's uncle's name was Obied Allah. These names reveal the personal devotion that Muhammad's pagan family had to the worship of Allah, the Moon god. His father died before he was born and his mother died while he was still young.

Many Christians have wrongly assumed that Allah was simply another name for the God of the Bible. Islam claims that Allah is the same God who was revealed in the Bible? This issue can only be decided by a comparison of the two documents in question.

When the son of Abdullah and Amina was born, he was named Muhammad. According to historical witnesses, Mohammad had a strange childhood, one marked by the presence of many different caretakers and "visitations" of spirits and angels.

We may gain an important insight into Mohammad from a description given of his mother. Muslim scholar Robert Morey writes," Muhammad's mother, Amina, was of an excitable nature and often claimed that she had been visited by spirits or jinns. She also at times claimed to have visions and religious experiences. Muhammad's mother was involved in what we call today the "occult arts" and this basic orientation is thought by some scholars to have been inherited by her son.

From birth, Amina feared for the infant's health in the crowded conditions of Mecca. So she did what Quraysh mothers with means customarily did- She hired a nurse from one of the Bedouin tribes to take him into "the healthy air of the desert".

Muhammad was entrusted to a Bedouin woman named Halima, who nursed the infant until he was two before bringing him back to Amina. Delighted with his healthy look, Muhammad's mother said "Take the child with thee back again, for much do I fear for him in the unwholesome air of Mecca. So Halima took him back. After two more years she returned again, but this time she was troubled. The child had experienced numerous fits, which made Halima think he was demon-possessed. Amina, however, pleaded with her to carry him back once more. But after subsequent epileptic fits and "spirit visitations", Halima returned him to his mother when he was five and refused to take him back. Muhammad always remembered Halima with great affection.

At the age of 25, Muhammad married Khadija who was widowed twice and had three daughters. Muhammad and Khadija had two sons, Abdullah, Qusam and a daughter named Fatima. Tragically the two boys died in infancy.
Muhammad exhibited mystic tendencies and was very religious from an early age.

Dr. Shorrosh gives this interesting description of Muhammad's appearance, based on eye witnesses' accounts. As an adult, Muhammad was somewhat above middle height with a lean but commanding figure. His head was massive, with a broad and noble forehead. He had thick black hair, slightly curled which hung over his ears, his eyes were large, black, and piercing; his eyebrows arched and joined; his nose was high and aquiline; and he had a long bushy beard. When he was excited, the veins would swell across his forehead; his eyes were often bloodshot and always restless. Decision marked his every movement. He used to walk so rapidly that his followers half ran behind him and could hardly keep up with him.

'The Night of Power'

In A.D 610 when Mohammad was 40, he had a visitation that would come to be known as "The Night of Power". It was this extraordinary experience that finally convinced Mohammad he was called to be God's Prophet and apostle. Muslims believe Allah began revealing true religion of Islam that night.

Testing Supernatural sources

The Bible offers tests to prove its authenticity as a message from God. Thus Moses, the first Prophet of God, was given a test to prove whether a message or a prophet was truly from God.

Deuteronomy 18:19-22

Here, God teaches that the true Prophet will make detailed Predictions about the future that can be proven or disproved. If the prophecies all come true, then the people are to heed his words as the word of God. If any part of his prophecy did not come true, they were to stone the person as a false prophet and destroy his message. If this test is applied today, most of the charismatic preachers would have been stoned to death by their own congregation.

This was the reason why, of all the books written in Israel's history, (and there were many), only the ones that were genuine were preserved in the canon of Scripture. And this was in spite of the fact that these books frequently condemned the people's sinful behavior from the king to the peasant. Each prophet proved himself true by fulfilled prophecy. The Israelites had every reason to destroy unpopular messages; some even predicted the destruction of the nation for its sin. But they did not dare destroy that which was proven to be God's word.

The Quran, on the other hand, has no such proofs with which to authenticate its divine origin. Instead, the believer is exhorted not to question and to kill anyone who does. Blind, unquestioning belief is demanded.

Islamic Revelation vs. Biblical Inspirations:

The concept of how the divine message of the Quran was received is very different form how the approximately 40 writers of the Bible received theirs. The Arabic word for "revelation" means 'handed down'. Muslims believe the Quran did not come "through" any man, not even Mohammad. They believe the message came directly from Allah to the angel Gabriel, who passed it to Mohammad as "a total Package," with no human involvement or interaction. Additionally, the Quran was not written down until years after Muhammad's death.

The Bible claims something very different about itself. It teaches that all scripture is "God breathed". The Bible further claims that it is not the product of man's interpretation 2 Peter 1:20-21, 2 Timothy 3:16-17.

The Bible is Unique

The great miracle of the Bible is that some forty authors from different times and places produced a Holy Book that has one homogenous, cohesive and consistent message. Its Divine origin is unmistakable. It does not contradict nature, history or any proven facts of science, though primitive men wrote it. The Bible contains hundreds of prophecies that have all been fulfilled with 100 percent accuracy and are historical records. No other book can compare with that record.

Muhammad begins to preach

According to early Muslim traditions the young pagan Muhammad experienced miraculous visions. Muhammad's mother Amina claimed that she was visited by spirits or Jinns. Some scholars think that Muhammad's early visions were the result of a combination of epileptic seizures and an over-active imagination. What must be remembered is that in the Arab culture of Muhammad's day, epileptic seizures were interpreted as a religious sign of either demonic possession or divine visitation. Muhammad thought that he was demon possessed and tried to commit suicide. But his devoted wife convinced him that he was not demon possessed. Although this information may offend many Muslims, we cannot simply ignore historical facts or seek to rewrite history in order to avoid hurting the feelings of those who do not want to hear the truth. Facts are facts regardless of how some one feels about them.

After the initial appearance of the angel, whom Muhammad later identified as Gabriel, Mohammad went through another period of self-doubt, depression and thoughts of death; He finally decided to commit suicide. He set out to end it all, but along the way he fell into another trance. While in the trance he had a vision in which he was told he must not end his life because he was truly called to be God's special messenger.

Khadija's Key Role

It is at this point that Khadija, Muhammad's wife played a pivotal role in his life. When he fully shared with her the anguish and doubt he had about his call from God, she strongly encouraged him.

She dismissed his fears of being demon-possessed as an absolute impossibility because he was such a good person. She vehemently believed that he was called by God as His Prophet and Apostle and kept assuring him of that. Khadija then urged Mohammad to begin preaching the message he received from the angel to his family and friends. All of his first converts were family members.

Opposition and Rejection

When the public heard about Mohammad's new teaching, opposition sprang up almost at once. The people of Mecca rejected and ridiculed his message. Even some family members turned against him.

Robert Morey explains the crisis that arose in Mohammad at this point,"In order to appease his pagan family members and the members of the Quraysh tribe, he decided that the best thing he could do was to agree with traditions that it was perfectly legitimate to pray to and worship the three daughters of Allah: Al-Lat, Al-Uzza, and Manat. Sura 53:19 This compromise led to the famous 'satanic verses' in which

Muhammad in a moment of weakness and supposedly under the inspiration of Satan succumbed to the temptation to appease the pagan mobs in Mecca.

The story of Mohammad's temporary appeasement of the pagans by allowing them their polytheistic practice cannot be ignored or denied. It is a fact of history. Only a few modern Muslim apologists reject the story of the "Satanic Verses" to avoid embarrassment.

The Yathrib Rebuke

Later, when the disciples of Yathrib (Medina) opposed this practice, Muhammad reverted back to the original message of monotheism saying Allah had now forbidden worship of the three goddesses. He explained this clear contradiction by saying that Allah could 'abrogate' or cancel a previous revelation.

Later Muhammad claimed that the angel Gabriel appeared to him and rebuked him for allowing Satan to deceive him into condoning the Meccan's worship of the three goddesses. So the revelations Muhammad received during this period were never included in the written version of the Quran. They came to be called "the Satanic Verses". Ayatollah Khomeini has issued a death sentence against Salman Rushdie for daring to write a book about these verses. The Meccans opposed Mohammad.

So, in A.D 622, with 200 followers, he fled to Medina, and it is known as the "Hegira".

Prophet and Apostle

At the age 40 Muhammad experienced once again a "Visitation". As a result of his experience, he ultimately claimed that Allah had called him to be a prophet and apostle. These two positions are unknown in Arabian tradition. The term Prophet was used in the hope that the Jews would accept Muhammad as a prophet, while the term apostle was likewise used in the hope that the Christians would acknowledge him as an apostle.

The Quran gives us four conflicting accounts of his original call to be a prophet. In the Quran Muhammad described his initial call to be a prophet and apostle on four different occasions. We are first told in Sura 53:2-18 and Sura 81:19-24 that Allah personally appeared to Muhammad in the form of a man and that Muhammad saw and heard him. This was later abandoned and we are told in Sura 16:102 and Sura 26:192-194 that Muhammad's call was issued by "The Holy Spirit". Since Muhammad doesn't discuss who or what this Holy Spirit was, this alleged call also was later abandoned. The third account of his original call is given in Sura 15:8 where we are told the Angels were the ones who came down to Muhammad and announced that Allah had called him to be a prophet. Even this account is later amended in Sura 2:97 so that it is only the angel Gabriel who issued the call to Muhammad. This last account in his original call was influenced by the fact that Gabriel had played a significant role in the birth of Jesus and John the Baptist. Muhammad assumed that it was only appropriate that the next great prophet in line, being himself, should also be issued the call by Gabriel. This fourth and last account of his initial call is the one that most Muslims and non-Muslims have known.

Chapter 6

Islam and Slavery

When we hear the word slavery, everyone in the world thinks about the slavery in America. Numerous books and movies have been produced in America, focusing on the brutality of slavery in America.

The famous movie "Roots" written by Alex Haley was released in 1976. It gained worldwide attention. The plot of Roots is about the capture, transportation, enslavement and brutality toward the black slaves that were transported to America. This movie made a great impact in all segments of the people. Black people became angrier and agitated and white people felt guiltier.

The American slavery was a small percentage of the slavery that took place throughout history. Although American slaves suffered, it benefited their descendants in America. Presently the American black population is better off than any other black people in the world, and they comprise around 13% of the US population.

In other countries slaves have no descendants because they perished without leaving any children. In the Middle East today you do not see any black population or also in South America, similar to the USA. The following section will be enlightening information about slavery.

Slavery existed throughout the world from time immemorial. The most dangerous threat to modern civilization and freedom is the rise of Islam. The majority of the people in the world know only the most rudimentary facts about this extraordinary potent and nefarious religious system. The conflict between Islam and the rest of the world may be the headline news in the world in 21st century. While everyone talks about American Slavery, surprisingly, little attention has been given to the Islamic slave trade in the Middle East, Asia and Africa. Whereas the Trans-Atlantic slave trade to the Americas lasted for just over three centuries, the Arab involvement in the slave trade has lasted fourteen centuries (1400 years). In some parts of the Islamic world, slavery is still practiced.

Facts

A comparison of the Islamic slave trade to the American slave trade reveals some interesting contrasts. While two out of every three slaves shipped across the Atlantic were men, the proportions were reversed in the Islamic slave trade. Two women for every man were enslaved by the Muslims. While the mortality rate for slaves being transported across the Atlantic was 10%, the percentage of slaves dying in transit in the Trans Sahara and East African slave trade was between 80 and 90%.

While almost all the slaves shipped across the Atlantic were for agricultural work, most of the slaves destined for the Muslim Middle East were for sexual exploitation as concubines, in harems, and for military service. While many children were born to slaves in the Americas and millions of their descendants are citizens in the USA to this day, the descendants under Islamic nations were very few or do not exist. In the USA black population is 14.6% of the total population. America even elected a black president, and many blacks are serving in prominent places in America.

While most slaves who went to America could marry and have families, most of the male slaves destined for the Middle East slave bazaars were castrated, and most of the children born to the women from them were killed at birth; because Muslim men did not want to raise the children from a slave woman. Imagine the gruesome scenes, before medical revolution in the primitive time; a knife is used without anesthesia for castrating men. Comparing the slaves in India and Africa, American slavery was more humane. It is estimated that possibly as many as eleven million Africans were transported across the Atlantic, 95% of which went to South and Central America, mainly to Portuguese, Spanish and French possessions. Only 5 percent of the slaves went to the United States.

However, at least 28 million Africans were enslaved in the Muslim Middle East. At least 80% of those captured by Muslim slave traders were calculated to have died before reaching the slave markets. It is believed that the death toll from the 14 centuries of Muslim slave trade into Africa could have been 112 million. When added to the number of those sold in the slave markets, the total number of African victims of the Trans Saharan and East African slave trade could be around 140 million.

Reformation

Christian Reformers spearheaded the anti-slavery movement in Europe and North America. Great Britain mobilized her Navy throughout most of the 19th century, to intercept slave ships and set the captives free. The Muslim religion never had a reformation. Great Britain outlawed the slave trade in 1807, and Europe abolished the slave trade in 1815, but Muslim slave traders enslaved another 2 million Africans. By some calculations the number of slaves for 14 centuries of Islamic slave trade could exceed 180 million.

Nearly 100 years after President Abraham Lincoln issued the Emancipation Proclamation in America and 130 years after all slaves within the British Empire were set free by Parliamentary decree, Saudi Arabia and Yemen, in 1962, and Mauritania in 1980, removed legalized slavery due to international pressure. Today slavery is prevalent in Islamic countries unofficially.

Pagan origin of slavery

Slavery predated Christianity, and many of the early Christians were slaves in the Roman Empire. The Pre-Christian world accepted slavery as normal and desirable. All the monuments of all civilizations were built on slave labor. Most of the slaves were white people, or Europeans. In fact, the very word "slave" comes from the people of Eastern Europe, the Slavs. The Latin term *sclāvus* originally referred to the Slavs of Eastern and Central Europe, as many of these people had been captured and then sold like chickens.

St. Patrick, the English Missionary to the Irish, was once a slave himself, kidnapped from his home and taken to Ireland against his will. Under Roman law, when a slave owner was found murdered, all his slaves were to be executed. In one case, when "Pedanius Secundas was murdered, all 400 of his slaves were put to death.

Before the coming of Jesus Christ, everyone in the world despised manual work and confined it to slaves. When Christ was born, half of the population of the Roman Empire were slaves. Three quarters of the population of Athens were slaves.

Slavery was indigenous to the African and Arab countries before it made its way to Europe. Slavery was widely practiced by the tribes of the American Indians long before Columbus set foot on the shores of the New World. What is seldom remembered or taught is that many black Americans in the 19th century owned slaves. For example, according to the United States census of 1830, in just one town of Charleston, South Carolina, 407 black Americans owned slaves themselves.

Christianity liberated slaves

Jesus revolutionized labor by taking up the axe, the saw, the hammer and the chisel. He endured labor with a new dignity. Christianity undercut slavery by giving dignity to work. By reforming work, Christianity transformed the entire social order. The Lord Jesus Christ began His ministry in Nazareth with this significant proclamation. (Luke 4.18) "The spirit of the Lord is upon me, because He has anointed me to preach the Gospel for the poor, He has sent me to heal the broken hearted, to proclaim liberty to the captives and recovery of sight to the blind, to set at Liberty those who are oppressed, to proclaim the acceptable year of the Lord". When the apostle Paul wrote to Philemon, concerning his escaped slave, he urged him to welcome back Onesimus. "No longer as a slave, but as a dear brother as a man and as a brother in the Lord": Philemon 16.

Because of these and other scriptural commands to love our neighbor, to be a Good Samaritan and do to others what you would want them to do to you, Christians like William Wilberforce, John Newton, William Carey, David Livingston, Lord Shaftesbury, Gen. Charles Gordon, Abraham Lincoln and many others worked tirelessly to end slavery and child labor. From the very beginning of the Christian church, Christians freed slaves.

During the second and third centuries many tens of thousands of slaves were freed by people who converted to Christ. Saint Melania emancipated 8000 slaves, Saint Ovidius freed 5000, Chromatius 1400 and Hermes 1200. Many Clergies at Hippo under Saint Augustine "freed their slaves as an act of piety." In AD 315 the Emperor Constantine, just two years after he issued the edict of Milan, legalizing Christianity, imposed the death penalty on those who stole children to bring them up as slaves.

Saint Augustine (AD 354-430) saw slavery as the product of sin and as contrary to God's Divine plan (The city of God). Saint Chrysostom in the 4th century taught that when Christ came, he annulled slavery. He proclaimed "in Christ Jesus there Is no slave, therefore it is not necessary to have a slave .... buy them and after you have taught them some skill by which they can maintain themselves, set them free."

The Islamic Slave Trade

With the birth of Islam came a rebirth of the slave trade. Ronald Segal in "Islam's Black slaves" documents, "when Islam conquered the Persian Sassanid Empire and much of the Byzantine Empire, including Syria and Egypt, it acquired immense quantities of gold stripping churches and monasteries either directly or by the taxes payable in gold, imposed on the clergy and looting gold from tombs. The state encouraged the search and sanctioned the seizure, in return for a fifth of the funds.

Segal notes "Female slaves were required in considerable numbers as musicians, singers and dancers, many more were bought for domestic workers and many were in demand, as concubines. "The harems of the rulers could be enormous. The harems of Abd Al Rahman 111 (912-961) in Cordoba contained over six thousand concubines. And the one in the Fatimid palace in Cairo had twice as many." Islam's Black Slaves also reveals that the castration of male slaves was common place. "The Caliph in Bagdad at the beginning of the 10th century had 7000 black eunuchs and 4000 white eunuchs in his palaces". It was noted that there was widespread "Homosexual relations" as well. Islam's black slaves notes that Islamic teachers throughout the centuries consistently defended slavery.

"For there must be masters and slaves". Others noted that Blacks "lack self-control and steadiness of mind and they are overcome by fickleness, foolishness and ignorance. Such are the Blacks who live in the extremity of the land of

Ethiopia, the Nubians, Zanj and the like". Ibn Khaldun, (1332-1406) the pre- eminent Islamic Medieval Historian and social thinker wrote: "the Negro nations are as a rule submissive to slavery because they have attributes that are quite similar to dumb animals".

By the Middle Ages, the Arab word "Abd "was in general use to denote a black slave, while the word "Mamluk" referred to a white slave. Even as late as the 19th century, it was noted that in Mecca there were few families that do not keep slaves, they all keep mistresses in common to their lawful wives". It was noted that Black slaves were castrated "based on the assumption that the Blacks had an ungovernable sexual appetite."

When the Fatimid came to power, they slaughtered all the tens of thousands black military slaves and raised an entirely new slave army. Some of these slaves were conscripted into the army at age 10. They were from Persia to Egypt to Morocco, numbering from 30,000 on up to 250,000. Even Ronald Segal, who favors Islam over Christianity, admits that well over thirty million Black Africans would have died at the hands of slave traders or ended up in Islamic Slavery.

The Islamic Slave trade took place across the Sahara Desert from the coast of the Red Sea, and from East Africa across the Indian Ocean. The Trans- Sahara Trade was conducted along six major slave routes. Just in the 19th century, for which we have more accurate records, 1.2 million slaves were brought across Sahara into the Middle East, 450,000 down the Red Sea and 442,000 from the East African coastal ports, that is a total of 2 million Black slaves just in the 1800s. At least 8 million more were calculated to have died before reaching the Muslim Slave market.

Islam's Black Slaves records: "In the 1570s a French man visiting Egypt found many thousands of Blacks on sale in Cairo on market days. In 1665, Father Antonios Gonzalis Spanish/ Belgian traveler, reported 800-1000 slaves on sale in the Cairo market on a single day. In 1776, a British traveler reported a caravan of 5000 slaves departing from Darfur. In 1838. It was estimated that 10,000 to 12,000 slaves were arriving in Cairo each year". Just in the Arabic plantations off the East coast of Africa, on the islands of Zanzibar and Pemba, there were 769,000 Black slaves. In the 19th century, the East African black slave trade included 347,000 slaves shipped to Arabia, Persia and India. 95,000 slaves were shipped to the Arab plantations in the Mascarem Islands.

Segal writes: The high death rate and low birth rate among black slaves in the Middle East and the astonishingly low birth rate amongst black slave women in North Africa and the Middle East decimated the black population. Islamic civilization lagged increasingly behind the west in protecting public health. The arithmetic of the Islamic black slave trade must also not ignore the lives of those men, women and children taken or lost during the procurement, storage and transport. The sale of a single captive for slavery might represent a loss of ten in the population from defenders killed in attacks on villages, the deaths of women and children from related famine and the loss of children, the old and sick, unable to keep up with their captors or killed along the way in hostile encounters, or dying of sheer misery".

Ronal Segal Islam's black slaves

One British explorer encountered over 100 human skeletons from a slave caravan en route to Tripoli. One caravan with 3000 proceeding from the coast in East Africa lost two thirds of its number from starvation, disease and murder. In the Nubian Desert, one slave caravan of 2000 slaves literally vanished as every slave died.

Eye Witness Account

In 1818, Captain Lyon of the Royal Navy reported that the Al-Mukani in Tripoli "waged war on all its defenseless neighbors and annually carried off 4000 to 5000 slaves, a piteous spectacle! These poor oppressed beings were many of them so exhausted as to be scarcely able to walk, their legs and feet were much swelled and by their enormous size formed a striking contrast with their emaciated bodies. They were all borne down with loads of firewood, and even poor little children worn to skeletons by fatigue and hardships, were obliged to bear their burden, while many of their inhumane masters with dreadful whip suspended from their waist.... all the traders speak of slaves as farmers do of cattle .... the defenseless state of the Negro Kingdoms to the southward are temptations too strong to be resisted, a force is therefore annually sent to pillage these defenseless people, to carry them off as slaves, burn their towns, kill the aged and infants, destroy their crops and inflict on them every possible misery. All slavery is for an unlimited time... None of their owners ever moved without their whips – which were in constant use ... drinking too much water, bringing too little wood or falling asleep before the cooking was finished, were considered nearby capital crimes, and it was in vain for these poor creatures to plead the excuse of being tired. Nothing could withhold the application of the whip. No slaves dared to be ill or unable to walk but when the poor sufferer dies, the master suspects that there must have been something wrong inside and regrets not having liberally applied their usual remedy of burning the belly with a red-hot Iron".

Christian Slaves

Segal also observed that: "white slaves from Christian Spain, Central and Eastern Europe were also shipped into the Middle East and served in the palaces of rulers and the establishments of the rich". He records that: "All Slavic eunuchs are castrated in that region and the operation is performed by Jewish merchants." Serge Trifkovic in "The Sword Of The Prophet" notes that in 781 AD, over 7000 Greeks were enslaved by the Muslims after they conquered Ephesus. When the Muslims captured Thessalonica in 903 AD, over 22,000 Christians were sold in to slavery. Similarly, in 1064 when Muslims invaded Georgia and Armenia they enslaved thousands of people.

The historian Otto Scott in his book "The Great Christian Revolution" details how Suleiman and his Turkish army of 300,000 invaded Hungary in 1526 and carried off 200,000 Hungarian Christians into slavery. In 1571, thousands of Greeks on Cypress were shipped to Constantinople as slaves.

Historian Robert Davies in his book "Christian slaves, Muslim masters - white slavery in the Mediterranean, the Barbary Coast and Italy", estimates that North African Muslim Pirates abducted and enslaved more than 1 million Europeans between 1530 and 1780. These Christians were seized in a series of raids which depopulated coastal towns from Sicily to Cornwall. Thousands of white Christians in coastal areas were seized every year to work as galley slaves, laborers and concubines for Muslim slave masters in what is known today as Morocco, Tunisia, Algeria, and Libya. Villages and towns on the coast of Italy, Spain, Portugal and France were the hardest hit, but the Muslim slave raiders also seized people as far afield as Britain, Ireland and Iceland.

According to one report, 7000 English travelers were abducted between 1622 and 1644; many of them were ship crews and passengers.

As the Ottoman Empire's ruling class degenerated into sensual overload, many of the intelligent kidnapped Christian boys from Europe came to play an increasingly important role as tutors, advisors, engineers and even Managers. Female captives were sexually abused in palace harems and others were held as hostages and bargained for ransom. Professor Davies estimates that up to 1.25 million Europeans were enslaved by Muslim slave traders between 1500 and 1800.

The European Slave Trade

While Islam dominated the slave trade from the 7th to the 15th century, between 1519 and 1815, Europe also joined in this trade in human flesh. The European nations who suffered most from Muslim slave raiders especially, Spain and Portugal dominated the European slave trade. During the Holy Roman Empire in 1519, Charles V who first authorized Europe's involvement into the slave trade. Britain's involvement in slavery was first authorized in 1631 by King Charles I (who was later executed by Parliament). His son, Charles II reintroduced it by Royal Charter in 1672. According to "The Slave Trade" by Hugh Thomas, approximately four million (35.4%) went to Portuguese controlled Brazil; 2.5 million slaves (22.1%) to the Spanish nations of South and Central America, 2 million (17.7%) to the British West Indies (most by Jamaica), 1.6 million (14.1%) to French West Indies; half a million (4.4%) to Dutch West Indies and half a million (4.4%) to North America.

The American Slave Trade

It is extraordinary considering that less than 5% of all the Trans-Atlantic Slaves ended up in North America, the vast majority of films, books and articles concerning the slave trade concentrate only on the American involvement as though slavery was a uniquely American aberration. However, the vastly great involvement of Portugal, Spain and France seems to be largely ignored. Even more so the far greater and longer running Islamic Slave Trade into the Middle East has been so ignored as to make it one of history's best kept secrets.

The African Slave Trade

The legends of European Slave Traders venturing into the jungles of Africa to capture free peoples are generally just that: Myths. The embarrassing fact of history is that the Europeans did not have to use any force to obtain these slaves. The slaves were "Sold" by their black owners. There was no need for the slave traders to risk their lives for venture into the jungles of Africa; they simply purchased the people from African chiefs and Muslim traders at the coast. However, while the slave trade and slavery was always criticized vigorously in Britain and America, no comparable criticism was evident in the Muslim Middle East or amongst the African tribes which sold their own people and neighboring tribes into slavery. Almost all of the African slaves transported across the Atlantic were captured and sold by African rulers and merchants. Every year, for about six hundred years the kingdom of Nubia (Sudan) was forced to send a tribute of slaves to the Muslims Sultan in Cairo.

Many tribal chiefs found it more profitable to sell their enemies, criminals and debtors than to kill or imprison them. Many were weaker neighboring tribes conquered for the express purpose of selling their people into slavery. The disgraceful fact is that there were three equally guilty partners in the crime of the Trans – Atlantic Slave trade. 1 Pagan African Tribal Chiefs, 2 Muslim Arabs and Christian Europeans were equally guilty. But Christians in Great Britain and USA put an end to the slavery. It is no accident that the most vicious terrorism originates from the least evangelized area of the world.

Untouchability in India is the worst form of slavery

Untouchability originated from the ancient Hindu religion and social systems. According to Traditional Hindu "Varna" system a person is born into one of the four castes based on Karma and purity. Those born as Brahmans are priest and teachers, Kshatriyas are rulers and soldiers, Vaishyas are merchants and traders and Sudras are laborers. Untouchables are literally outcastes. They are not included in any of the traditional Varna or caste system of the Hindu religion. According to Dr. Amberkar, untouchables form an entirely new class i.e. the fifth Varna apart from the existing four castes.

Around 200 million people in India are considered "untouchable"- people tainted by their birth into a cast system that deems them impure and less than human. Once these untouchables were not allowed to drink from the same well, attend the same temples, wear shoes in the presence of an upper class or drink from the same cups.

They are relegated to the lowest jobs and lived in constant fear of being publically humiliated, paraded naked, beaten and raped with impunity by upper class Hindus seeking to keep them in their place. Merely walking through an upper cast neighborhood was a life threatening offence. Despite the fact that untouchability was officially banned when India adopted its constitution in 1950, discrimination against the low caste remained so pervasive that in 1989 the Government passed the legislation known as "The prevention of Atrocities Act 1989." The Act specifically made it illegal to parade people naked through the streets, force them to eat feces, take away their land, foul their water, and burn down their homes, and interfere with their right to vote. In rural India the above mentioned incidents happen even today.

The people of Kerala in South India practiced the worst form of untouchability in the world. Swami Vivekananda a Hindu sage, reformer and philosopher called Kerala a" lunatic asylum".
This quote is from Vivekananda's work "the Future of India"

"Was there ever a sillier thing before in the world than what I saw in Malabar country? The poor Pariah is not allowed to pass through the same streets as the high cast man but if he changes his name to a hodge-podge English name, it is alright; or to a Mohammedan name. It is alright. What inference would you draw except that these Malabaris are all lunatics, their homes so many lunatic asylums"

A Nair (a middle class caste) could behead a low caste person if he touched him and a similar fate awaited a slave, who did not turn out off the road as the Nair passed. According to Kerala tradition, low caste people were forced to maintain a distance of 64 feet from a high caste, as they were thought to pollute them. Based on caste hierarchy, some were to keep distances of 72 feet, 32 feet and 24 feet respectively. Even in the beginning of the twentieth century, the high caste men when walking along the road uttered a warning grunt or hoot to person of any lower castes to keep enough distance. Lower caste people had no right to tile their house, to build an upstairs building, or a gateway. No man could approach him with more than a single cloth around his waist which shouldn't fall below his knees. If a man of lower caste were by misfortune to touch a Nair lady her relatives would immediately kill her and the man who touched her and all his relatives. Low caste people when speaking expected to cover their mouth, using in conversation a self-depreciating form of speech with special standardized servile expressions and submissive bodily postures.

The British outlawed most of the outrageous practices Breast Tax (Mulakkaram)

This is the story of a low caste Hindu woman who lived in the 19th century in a place called "Cherthala" in Kerala, South India. The state government had imposed a breast tax on low caste Hindu woman called "Mulakkaram" (Breast Tax). which was to be paid so that they could cover their breasts. Upper caste women could cover their breasts without paying any tax. In 2012 Kerala observed the 200th anniversary of the end of the breast tax. The following facts are from an article published in "The Hindu" on October 21,

2013 by Nidhi Surendra Nath. Nangeli, who lived in Chertala in Allappuzha over 200 years ago, gained her place in history as the woman who cut off her breasts to protest against the inhuman Mulakkaram (breast tax) that was imposed in the erstwhile kingdom of Travancore (Kerala).

Caste Oppression

Kings of the time ensured the subjugation of the lower caste by imposing heavy taxes on them. Their wealth was built on some of the worst taxes imposed anywhere in the world. Besides the tax on land and crops, peasants had to pay taxes for the right to wear jewelry, the right of men to grow a moustache and even the right of women to cover their breast. (There were a hundred similar silly taxes.) The three upper castes had tax exempt status. Colonel John Munroe removed all taxes for the poor low caste people and taxed all the upper caste people. This invited a great uproar against John Munroe from the upper caste people.

The heavy taxes ensured that the lower castes were kept eternally in debt while members of the upper caste flourished. Nangeli was a poor Ezhava woman from Chertala. Her family could not afford to pay the taxes and was in debt to the rulers. The Tax Collector then called "Pravathiar came to her house to demand tax because she covered her breast. Then Nangeli cut off one of her breasts and presented it to the Tax collector". The Tax Collector fled in fear while Nangeli bled to death at her door step. Her husband, Mr. Kandappan who was away during the incident, after returning jumped on her funeral pyre and died. The very next day the tax was withdrawn by the Sree Mulam Thirunal, Maharaja of Travancore, fearing public agitation.

In Kerala, the British Ruler Colonel Munroe reformed Kerala society.

From Wikipedia

"John Munro was born in June 1778, second son of Captain James Munro, 7th of Teaninich (Royal Navy).

Military career

John Munro, 9th of Teaninich entered the army at an early age and was sent to Madras where he took part in the battle of Seringapatam and was shortly afterwards appointed Adjutant of his regiment, in which office he displayed a thorough acquaintance with military duties. John Munro also became an accomplished linguist, being able to speak and write fluently in French, German, Italian, Arabic, Persian and several of the Indian dialects.

John Munro held various appointments on the Staff, and was private secretary and interpreter to successive Commanders in Chief in India. He was personally acquainted and in constant correspondence with Colonel Arthur Wellesley, Duke of Wellington during the Maratha war, John Munro assisted in quelling the Nellore Mutiny and was soon afterwards appointed Quartermaster-General of the Madras army, at the early age of twenty-seven.

Administrative career and Legacy

Col. John Munro distinguished himself well in the field, and had a talent for handling the Indian people. His tactful handling of the people of Travancore and the kingdom of Cochin at a time of the attack by Velu Thampi Dalawa on the East India Company, led to his being appointed the Resident of the Company for these kingdoms. Col. Munro also served as the Diwan (Prime Minister) to the Regents Rani Gouri Lakshmi Bai and Rani Gouri Parvati Bai of the kingdom of Travancore and Raja Kerala Varma of the kingdom of Cochin from 1812 to 1818. With this freedom of action, he won the confidence of the rulers and the people as to be able to introduce the practice, in the administration of justice, of having a Christian sitting on the bench as judge beside a Brahmin. Nothing in his career so marked him as a great administrator; he saw what other men failed to see for a long time after that, the British and Indians learned the secret of true co-operation. He was instrumental in influencing these rulers to introduce a large number of progressive reforms. During his tenure as the Diwan of these states, he reformed the judicial system, improved the revenue of the states, prevented corruption and mismanagement and started the process of abolishing slavery in 1812. Slavery was abolished in the Munroe Island on the 8th of March 1835 and finally by Royal proclamations by the maharajah of Travancore in 1853 and 1855. He removed many of the irksome taxes levied on the poorer sections of the community. Despite being the resident of the English East India Company, during differences of opinion between the English East India Company and Travancore or Cochin, he always argued in favor of the princely states. Col. John Munro faced severe criticism and official censure by the methods which he was bold enough to adopt, but he proved the true wisdom of his plan, by making it work to the benefit of the governors and the governed. He lived to see Muslims and high caste Hindus appreciate the integrity and fairness of Christian judges, and he paved the way for those who since his day have tried to interpret Western Christianity to the

Eastern people. For these reasons, he was adored by the people of these kingdoms and an archipelago of eight islands located in the Ashtamudi Lake, called the Munroe Island, has been named in honor of Col. John Munro. History has recorded that Col. John Munro was one of the most brilliant and popular administrators of Travancore and Cochin." In Kerala Hindu temples became bankrupt due to corruption, nepotism and incompetence. Colonel Munroe, the British Resident, appointed in 1812 as Diwan of the Cochin and Travancore kingdoms, was responsible for bringing effective controls on temples. Munroe recommended that all Devaswom properties be treated as government properties and the revenue from Devaswom be merged with the general revenues of the state. In addition, for the purpose of meeting the expenses of the temples, *Pathiv* (that is, a scale of expenditure on uthsavams, remuneration to temple staff, maintenance charges etc.) was proposed. These recommendations were accepted by the maharajas of Cochin and Travancore. A committee was constituted to study its implications in 1815. During the reign of Maharani Gowri Parvati Ba in Travancore, a royal decree was passed forming a Devaswom Board, and most of the temples in Travancore were brought under its control." So John Munroe not only reformed Christianity but helped the Hindu religion to prosper.

Instead of blaming America for the past slavery, try to learn the true history of slavery in the world. Everyone in the world was guilty of the same sin in the worst order.

The Positive Aspects of American Slavery.

There are two most despicable words in the world today. These two words are "colonialism and slavery.

The first thing we should realize is that the entire world was barbaric until the end of the Second World War. Isolated barbarism and brutality will prevail in the world until the end of the world. For example, we saw the genocide in Rwanda the destruction of the half of the population of Cambodia by Pol Pot and the unspeakable brutalities of ISIS. The present day black population in America blame past slavery for all their maladies. Let us see the real facts. The black population should be grateful for the slavery. What happened to the black people who stayed behind in Africa many centuries ago? We all know that Africa always had tribal war and it still continue in many countries in Africa. Death rate in Africa was very high due to malnutrition and tribal warfare in the previous centuries Conversely, American slaves had healthier and longer lives in America. Protestant slave masters treated the slaves in a more humane fashion, but many others treated the slaves very harshly. Slavery was prevalent throughout the world from time immemorial. If you compare slavery in India, the American slavery was like a picnic for blacks.

Segregation of blacks

According to Wikipedia you can assess the facts about discrimination in the USA.

"**Jim Crow laws** were state and local laws enforcing racial segregation in the Southern United States. Enacted after the Reconstruction period, these laws continued in force until 1965. They mandated *de jure* **racial segregation** in all public facilities in states of the former Confederate States of America, starting in 1890 with a "separate but equal" status for African Americans. Conditions for African Americans were consistently inferior and underfunded compared to those available to white Americans. This body of law institutionalized a number of economic, educational, and social disadvantages. *De jure* segregation mainly applied to the Southern United States, while Northern segregation was generally *de facto* — patterns of housing segregation enforced by private covenants, bank lending practices, and job discrimination, including discriminatory labor union practices.

Jim Crow laws mandated the segregation of public schools, public places, and public transportation, and the segregation of restrooms, restaurants, and drinking fountains for whites and blacks. The U.S. military was also segregated, as were federal workplaces, initiated in 1913 under President Woodrow Wilson, the first Southern president elected since 1856. By requiring candidates to submit photos, his administration practiced racial discrimination in hiring.

These Jim Crow laws followed the 1800–1866 Black Codes, which had previously restricted the civil rights and civil liberties of African Americans. Segregation of public (state-sponsored) schools was declared unconstitutional by the Supreme Court of the United States in 1954 in *Brown v. Board of Education*. Generally, the remaining Jim Crow laws were overruled by the Civil Rights Act of 1964 and the Voting Rights Act of 1965, However, years of action and court challenges were needed to unravel numerous means of institutional discrimination."

Discrimination in any form is wrong and sinful, but the real fact is that only the white Christians corrected the injustice in the world. Even today we can see the barbaric and brutal slavery in Muslim countries. In 2015, half of the Syrian people fled Syria to escape from the civil war. Where did they go? We all know that the Middle East Arab countries are very rich, and have a vast area of land , but they have not admitted a single refugee from Muslim countries. Although most Asians, Africans, and Middle easterners hate Capitalism and white Christians, when they lost everything they opted to go to Europe or America. It means inside their heart they know that white Christians are better than their own Muslim brothers.

Now let us examine American slavery. After the Arabs sold blacks to American whites, there were millions of blacks left in Africa. How was their condition in Africa? Even in the 21st century there are tribal conflicts in most of Africa. What was the condition in Africa 400 years ago?

Tribal and civil wars were extremely brutal at that time. Most of the blacks who stayed back in Africa perished from tribal wars, malnutrition and diseases. At the same time those who came to America received food, and shelter although they had to work very hard. The white man taught them English, and gave them the gospel, and they became very strong Christians with a blessed hope. Their children became better than their counterparts in Africa. Yes, they had to sit in the back of the bus. It was really bad. At the same time, they had the right to ride in the same bus. Imagine in India a low caste person had to be 60 to 90 feet away from a high cast person. Yes, blacks had a separate water fountain, but still their life in America was a thousand times better than their counterparts in Africa. They didn't have even donkeys or horses to ride. They had to walk without water or food. Yes, the White Christians in America made amends for their sins. Today blacks should be grateful about the blessing of Slavery.

Let me quote Walter Williams, one of the eminent economists in the world.

"Black Americans, compared with any other racial groups, have come the greatest distance, over some of the highest hurdles, in a shorter period of time. This unprecedented progress can be verified through several measures. If one were to total black earnings and consider black Americans a separate nation, he would find that, in 2008, they earned $726 billion. That would make them the world's sixteenth-richest nation, just behind Turkey but ahead of Poland, the Netherlands, Belgium, and Switzerland." Walter E. Williams. Race & Economics. Hoover Institution, Press. Page 5.

Who gets more Olympic medals for generations? American blacks.

Colonialism

Before the Partition of India in 1947, 562 of **Princely States**, also called **Native States**, existed in India, which was not part of British India. These were the parts of the Indian subcontinent which had not been conquered or annexed by the British, but were subject to subsidiary alliances.

From history we know that hundreds of independent countries never got along, which facilitated Islamic countries to come to India and subjugate the population for centuries. If British never came to India, it would have become an Islamic country like Saudi Arabia which practice strict Sharia law. The British came and united India which became one of the powerful countries of the world in the twenty-first century. Today India has 350million English speaking population, and are enjoying the fruits of Colonialism.

Colonialism existed from the beginning of man. World history is full of examples of one society gradually expanding by incorporating adjacent territory and settling its people on newly conquered territory. The Babylonians, the Persians, the Greeks, and the Romans, captured and colonized most territories in the world at different periods in history. Colonialism, then, is not restricted to a specific time or place. Nevertheless, in the sixteenth century, colonialism changed decisively because of technological developments in navigation that began to connect more remote parts of the world. Fast sailing ships made it possible to reach distant ports and to sustain close ties between the center and colonies. Thus, the modern European colonial project emerged when it became possible to move large numbers of people across the ocean and to maintain political sovereignty in spite of geographical dispersion. This entry uses the term colonialism to describe the process of European settlement and political control over the rest of the world, including the Americas, Australia, and parts of Africa and Asia. Most people in the world think that Colonialism was one of the greatest sins in the world. Actually colonialism is the single reason for the technological progress of the present world.

In India, everyone says that the British came to India and plundered its wealth. The British rule started around 1600 and lasted until 1947. Of course they came to make money; that is latent in every human being.

Dadabhai Naoroji, The Benefits of British Rule, 1871

An intellectual, educator, and merchant, Dadabhai Naoroji (1825-1917) was known as the "Grand Old Man of India." As a Member of Parliament (1892-95) in the House of Commons in Britain, and as a co-founder of the Indian National Congress, Naoroji acquired much experience in the political process and in dealing with the British, who occupied India since the 18th century. Among his many roles was as a professor of mathematics and natural philosophy at Mumbai, India as well as a professor of languages at the University College, London.

The Benefits of British Rule for India*:*

***"In the Cause of Humanity*:** Abolition of *suttee* and infanticide. Destruction of *Dacoits, Thugs, Pindarees*, and other such pests of Indian society. Allowing remarriage of Hindu widows, and charitable aid in time of famine. Glorious work all this, of which any nation may well be proud, and such as has not fallen to the lot of any people in the history of mankind.

***In the Cause of Civilization*:** Education, both male and female. Though yet only partial, an inestimable blessing as far as it has gone, and leading gradually to the destruction of superstition, and many moral and social evils. Resuscitation of India's own noble literature, modified and refined by the enlightenment of the West.

Politically: Peace and order. Freedom of speech and liberty of the press. Higher political knowledge and aspirations. Improvement of government in the native states. Security of life and property. Freedom from oppression caused by the caprice or greed of despotic rulers, and from devastation by war. Equal justice between men and men (sometimes vitiated by partiality to Europeans). Services of highly educated administrators, who have achieved the above-mentioned results.

Materially: Loans for railways and irrigation. Development of a few valuable products, such as indigo, tea, coffee, silk, etc. Increase of exports. Telegraphs.

Generally: A slowly growing desire of late to treat India equitably, and as a country held in trust. Good intentions. No nation on the face of the earth has ever had the opportunity of achieving such a glorious work as this. I hope in the credit side of the account I have done no injustice, and if I have omitted any item which anyone may think of importance, I shall have the greatest pleasure in inserting it. I appreciate, and so do my countrymen, what England has done for India, and I know that it is only in British hands that her regeneration can be accomplished. Now for the debit side. "There is no doubt that the British also benefitted enormously. India was ruled by more than 500 princely kingdoms that never worked together but actually fought each other.

Today, the Indian community is very prominent in Africa, the Caribbean islands, Middle East and America. The present generation of Indians are deriving the benefit of British Colonialism. Many Indians proudly send chain email and Facebook postings showing the intellectual prowess of Indians in America.

According to them, and many other surveys, the following facts are given:

38 Percent of doctors in US are Indians

36 percent of NASA scientists are Indians.

34 percent of Microsoft employees are Indians

28 percent IBM employees are Indians.

17 percent of Intel employees are Indians

12 percent of total scientists in US are Indians.

We don't have the number for Indians working for Apple, Google and Facebook.

Indians are the chief executives of Google and Microsoft. Facebook employs numerous Indians.

Google and Microsoft Company are led by Indians.

If British never came to India, the Indians would still be living in the dark ages.

Chapter 7

Sex in Islamic Heaven

Muhammad had two great weaknesses. The first was greed; by looting caravans and Jewish settlements, he had amassed fabulous wealth for himself, his family, and his tribe.

His next greatest weakness was women. Although in the Quran he would limit his followers to having four wives, he himself took more than four wives and concubines. Muslim scholar and statesman Ali Dashti gives the following list of the women in Muhammad's life.

1 Khadija
2 Sawda
3 Aisha
4 Omm Salama
5 Hafsa
6 Zaynab (of Jahsh)
7 Jowayriya
8 Omm Habiba

9 Safiya
10 Maymuna (of Hareth)
11 Fatima
12 Hend
13 Asma of Saba)
14 Zaynab (of Khozayma)
15 Habla
16 Asma 9 of Norman
17 Mary (The Christian)
18 Rayhana
19 Omm Sharik
20 Maymuna
21 Zaynab (a third one)
22 Khawla

The first 16 women were wives. Numbers 17 and 18 were slaves or concubines. The last four women were neither wives nor slaves but devout Muslim women who gave themselves to satisfy Muhammad's sexual desires. One day Muhammad went out to look for Zaid, Muhammad's adopted son). Now there was a covering of cloth over the doorway, but the wind had lifted the covering so that the doorway was uncovered. Zaynab was in her chamber, undressed, and admiration for her entered into the heart of the prophet. The admiration was noticed by Zaynab. She mentioned it to her husband Zaid later. He rushed to his father's house and offered Zaynab to him. According to history, Allah sanctioned the marriage. Another wife Aisha was only eight or nine years old when Muhammad took her to his bed. Muhammad's sexual activities were legendary. The Hadiths make the claim that he was able to have sex with all of them every day before prayers. He supposedly had the sexual strength of thirty men. Such claims were made to impress the Arabs, who at the time believed that ceaseless sexual activity was paradise. Narrated Qatadah: Anas bin Malik said "The prophet used to visit all his wives in a round, during the day and the night and they were eleven in number. I asked Anas "Had the prophet strength for it". Anas replied, "We used to say that the prophet was given the strength of thirty men". Vol: 1, No.268. Aisha said, "I scented Allah's prophet and he went around (had sexual relation with) all his wives." Vol: 1, 270 and No, 267

Do you know why suicide deaths by Muslim jihadists are exploding recently? Another interesting factor is that the suicide murderers are usually between the ages 15 and 40. Although Yasser Arafat sent many suicide bombers to kill Israeli school children and other civilians, he or any old Jihadists never volunteered to die. This truth is well known. Bin Laden, Ayatollah Khomeini and all other senior extremists brainwashed and enticed young men to commit suicide for Allah. So these young Muslims are motivated to terrorism because the Quran tells them that fighting non-believers is a duty and they will go to heaven to enjoy untold sensual pleasures. If they can make it to heaven the Muslims martyrs are promised 72 virgins. The number of virgins is not specified in the Quran; it comes from a quotation of Muhammad recorded in one of the lesser known Hadith. Muhammad knew that sex would sell very well among the group of his followers who were motivated to fight battles by the promise of sex slaves and booty. The specific Hadith in which the number of virgins is specified is hadith Al- Tirmidhi in the book of Sunnah (Volume 1V, chapter 21,

Islam blames America and the west for all sexual immorality including homosexuality, pornography etc. When former Iranian president Mahmoud Ahmadinejad visited America, he stated that there were no homosexuals in Iran. Even today if somebody is caught for adultery, people in the Islamic world stone him/her to death. So outwardly there is a semblance of great morality. However, watching sex movies engaging in homosexual acts secretly is very common in Islamic countries.

Boys in Heaven

"The prophet Muhammad was heard saying: The smallest reward for the people of paradise is an abode where there are 80,000 servants and 72 wives, over which stands a dome decorated with pearls, aquamarine, and ruby, as wide as the distance from Al-Jabiah (a Damascus suburb) to Sana'a (Yemen), but modern apologists reject the homosexual pleaser in heaven to avoid embarrassment. Homosexuality was and is widely practiced in Islamic countries. To please the homosexual followers of Muhammad he promised them pre-pubescent boys in paradise. Quran 52:24 "And there will go round boy-servants of theirs, to serve them as if they were preserved pearls." Sura.6:17. "They will be served by immortal boys." 76:19 "And round about them will (serve) boys of everlasting youth. If you see them, you would think them scattered pearls." Sura 47:15 narrates 'Rivers of milk and wine, and honey" in Paradise.

The supreme leader of Iran, the Shia Grand ayatollah Ruhollah Khomeini, in 1979-89 sanctioned sexual relation even with a child. Read" Khomeini, "Tahrirolvasyleh" fourth volume, Darol ELM, GOM, Iran, 1990.

The Quran promises a heaven full of wine and free sex. Sura 2:25; 4:57; 11:23; 47:15. If drunkenness and gross immorality is sinful on earth, how is it right in Paradise? This is another proof that Islam reflects the ideas and customs of seventh-century Arab culture. The Quran's picture of paradise is exactly what a seventh- century pagan Arab would have thought wonderful. The Islamic utopia presents a beguiling theory of carnal gratification catering to the secret desire of men to have sex with willing young girls. Muhammad held that sexual urges do not perish with death.

In order to understand the nature of sex in the Islamic Utopia, one must understand the nature of Islam's sex slave "The Houri". Houris are young, nymphs who were created for one purpose only. They exist to be sexual servants to men. The life of a Houri is a submissive one just as the life of Muslims who must submit to Allah. Allah created Houris to serve Muslim men; therefore, they do not know a world outside this sexual servitude. In the Hadiths Muhammad gave all the believers a choice between open sex markets, where there would be no limit to the number of sexual partners they could have. Hadith: Al hadiths. Vol 4 page 172, No 34

"A Houri is a most beautiful young woman with a transparent body. The marrow of her bones is visible like the interior lines of pearls and rubies. She looks like red wine in a white glass. She is of white color, and free from the routine physical disabilities of an ordinary woman who are subjects to such periodic bodily changes as menstruation, menopause, urinal and offal discharge, childbearing and the related pollution. A Houri is a girl of tender age, having large breasts, which are rounded (Pointed) and not inclined to dangle". Tirmzi. Volume two (P35-40) According to this, a black woman can never be a Houri. You are talking about racism in paradise. Different hadiths give detailed accounts of sexual relations. The description of paradise in Quran is given below Sura 47:15;52;17-20; 37:40-48; 44:51-55; 55:56-

57; 55:72; 78:31-32; 78:33-34; 55:72; 78:31-32; 78:33-34; 55:57-58; 55:34-37; 55:70-77; 56:22; 56:35-36; 55:56; 2:25 The above text from “The Islamic sex slave in Paradise” by Naomi Chambers.

Chapter 8

Ayatollah Khomeini on Sex

Ayatollah Ruhollah Khomeini, wrote extensively on Islamic Jurisprudence. A two-volume book, which was published originally in Arabic, was called 'Tahrir al Wasilah'. Translated into Farsi, the book is called "Tahrirolvasyleh." (Read entire text here.) Khomeini also had another treatise on Islamic rules for living, called in English, "The Little Green Book." (See entire text here.) "The Little Green Book of Ayatollah Khomeini is Translated from Persian by Daniel Deleanu, MA, MLitt, PhD. Published by Logo Star Press Toronto. 2011

It is useful to understand what an esteemed Islamic leader such as the Ayatollah teaches his followers. Here are some excerpts from the "Tahrirolvasyleh" which Muslims probably don't want you to know:

Ayatollah Khomeini has sanctioned sex even with animals. Read 'The little Green Book of Ayatollah Khomeini' Translated from Persia by Daniel Deleanu. Page78.

Wine and all intoxicating beverages are impure, but opium and hashish are not.

A woman who has contracted a continuing marriage does not have the right to go out of the house without her husband's permission; she must remain at his disposal for the fulfillment of any one of his desires, and may not refuse herself to him except for a pertinent reason, such as a religious one.

Pedophilia legal in Iran

In June, 2002, Iranian authorities approved a law raising the age at which girls can marry without parental consent from 9 to 13. The elected legislature actually passed the bill in 2000, but the "Guardian Council", a 12-man body of conservative clerics, vetoed it as contradicting Islamic Sharia law. Iran's clerical establishment insists that the marriage of young girls is a means to combat immorality. The Expediency Council, which arbitrates between the elected parliament and the theocratic Guardian Council, timidly passed the measure. The law, however, does not change the age at which children can get married (nine for girls and 14 for boys), but says that girls below the age of 13 and boys younger than 15 need their parents' permission and the approval of a "Righteous Court." Reformists state that the new law does not protect children, since most of those who marry at such a young age do so by force.

JUST DISCOVERED, ISIS Charges People $172 to Have Sex with One-Year-Old Infants and Nine-Year-Old Children (READ THE NEW PRICE LIST ISIS JUST RELEASED)
By Shoebat Foundation on November 4, 2014 in Featured, General
By Walid Shoebat (Shoebat Exclusive)

ISIS has set up the standard market price list for the sale of sex slaves. Yes, you got it right. It's right here in black and white and blue (the ISIS seal of approval):

And we will translate it verbatim for all you English readers who still say that the sale of women is not true Islam:

"Price List–Sale of Booty

"We have been informed that the market for sale of women had been witnessing a reduction in price, which affects the needs for the Islamic State and the funding for the Mujahideen. For this, the commerce department has decided to set a fixed price regarding the sale of women. Therefore, all auctioneers are to abide by this and anyone who breaks the rules will be executed.

PRICE (in Dinar)	MERCHANDISE
75,000	age 30-40/Yezidi/Christian
100,000	age 20-30/Yezidi/Christian
150,000	age 10-20/Yezidi/Christian
50,000	age 40-50/Yezidi/Christian
200,000	age 1-9/Yezidi/Christian

Limit to 3 Sex Slaves with exception to foreign sales to Turks, Syrians and the Gulf states".

The price reduction issued by ISIS was to expedite the sale of sex slaves due to an overstock. Clients from Turks, Syrians and the Gulf states can purchase more than 3 sex slaves from an array of mature women, young women, teens, under age ... to even infants. The conversion rate is $86 dollars for 100,000 Iraqi dinars.

The sources from the Middle East report thousands of innocent Christian and Yezidi women come in the forefront involving rape, kidnapping and murder, flogging and stoning and forced marriages.

Countless sources reported the new deal; the prettiest of women for sale in the slave market are distributed to the ISIS princes while others are murdered for refusing to practice Sex Jihad. The Mehr (dowry) for women in "Nineveh" Iraqi province could reach up to one and a half million dinars. Any woman who resists is given 30 lashes, and all sales outside the Muslim courts in the province are prohibited.

Westerners think that bizarre sex dealings are only restricted to ISIS. Misyar marriage, for example, is nothing more than legalized call girls and has branches globally including in the U.S. It was first sanctioned in Egypt and Saudi Arabia and it spread to several other Muslim nations. There are many websites used to facilitate the transactions. The most popular is click here for 'lonely' Muslim men who are on the road and are allowed to have sex with local Muslim women (who advertise themselves) in the area where the lonely Muslim male is traveling where he can order his bride in the comfort of his hotel room by the touch of his keyboard.

Mesiara Online screenshot

Call girls are permitted in Islam and even with Muslim women donned with Hijabs. Misyar means sex for the travelers. While prostitution exists in every corner of the globe, its sanctification with fanciful words is what is particularly at issue here. The word prostitution is stealthily removed since there is a transaction established that says "marriage" instead.

Misyar is all over the Middle East and is sanctioned by many top Imams. The Muslim "conservative" world is much more disgusting than one can imagine. It's actually far more like western liberalism than western conservatism. Misyar marriages are rarely if ever discussed in Western mainstream media, perhaps – at least in part – for that reason.

ISIS simply follows the Muslim standards set by Imams in Saudi Arabia and Egypt. Kurdish intelligence states that thousands of abducted women work as slaves in homes or are being sold to human traffickers to work in brothels in several parts of the Middle East, while others are forced to marry ISIS fighters. Officers in the Kurdish intelligence report that women are sold to people smugglers for prices that range between $ 500 and $ 3000. Some women were abductees from the town of Sinjar, while thousands were kidnapped from nearby towns and villages. Schools in Tal Afar are used for temporary holding places for women.

A spokesman for the Iraqi Red Crescent, Mohammed al-Khuzai, declared that "elements of the organization of ISIS detained dozens of Yazidi and Christian families at Tal Afar Airport. They killed all the men and carried their wives to the markets to be sold as sex slaves." He pointed out that Christians and Yazidis were stranded in the mountains in Sinjar, numbering 200 thousand displaced people, including more than 25 thousand children, and noted that the delivery of assistance to them was difficult because the roads were closed. Recently trading pioneers of social networking sites showed hundreds of video clips, which explained the prices for Yezidi and Christian sex slaves.

Shoebat.com was the first to show a leaked video of ISIS auctioneers discussing the distribution of sex slaves:
The video shows ISIS openly admitting the establishment of a "slave market" to sell sex slaves.

Times of India April 22-2015

Sharia compliant' sex shop to open in Mecca selling halal sex products

Lizzie Dearden, The Independent | Apr 22, 2015, 03.53 PM IST.

Thousands of Muslims gather around the holy Kaaba during evening prayer in the holy city of Mecca. (File Photo)
A "Sharia compliant" sex shop is reportedly set to open in Mecca selling halal products and toys.
El Asira, an erotic brand originating in Amsterdam, is branching out to Islam's holiest city in Saudi Arabia, visited by millions of Muslims a year on the "hajj" pilgrimage.
Founder Abdelaziz Aouragh announced his ambition last year, and now the shop is almost ready to open, Morocco-based website Alyaoum24 reported. Muslim clerics and Saudi sheikhs have reportedly been consulted to ensure the business complies with local laws and customs.

Mecca under threat: Outrage over plan to destroy the 'birthplace' of prophet Muhammad.

"The products we're putting on the market have nothing to do with blow-up dolls or vibrators," Mr. Aouragh told the AFP news agency. "It's not about the sex act, it's what's going on around it. Our products increase the atmosphere and heighten feelings of sensuality." Women's freedoms are severely restricted in Saudi Arabia, and Islamic codes of behavior and dress are strictly enforced, but El Asira says it strives to lead to "more admiration and love for women" by improving marital relationships. Its website describes all products as "Sharia compliant" and claims they can "provide a deeper meaning to sexuality, sensuality and even spirituality".

Everything sold online and in the brand's shops has been deemed "halal", meaning they are permissible according to Islamic law. "All our products are maintaining the integrity, pure humanity and ethics inherent with the Sharia," the website says. The company, launched in the Netherlands in 2010, specializes in sensual oils and is backed by the German adult company Beate Uhse.

Chapter 9

Muhammad a White Man

Hadith clearly states that Muhammad was a White man. This is stated so many times in so many ways that it is quite obvious that the authors of the hadith were deeply concerned that someone may think that Muhammad was a black man. This will come as quite a shock to the Black Muslims in America who have claimed that Islam is a black man's religion because Muhammad was a black man. Now we know that Black Muslims in America belong to a white man's religion.

In Sahih Al Bukhari vol. 1 no. 63, we read "while we were sitting with the Prophet, a man came and said, "who amongst you is Mohammed?" We replied, "**this white man** reclining on his arm..."

In volume 2 Hadith no. 122 refers to Mohammed as a "**white person**" and in vol. 2 Hadith no. 141 we are told that when Mohammed raised his arms, "**the whiteness** of his armpits became visible.".

Arab racism in the Quran

According to the literal translation of Sura 3: 106-107 from the Arabic version, on judgment day, only people with white faces will be saved. People with black faces will be damned. This is racism in the worst form. American blacks have been widely wooed by Islam, but through misinformation. They hear, "Christianity is the White man's religion; Islam is the religion of all mankind". They are told that Allah and Muhammad are black. In reality, Muslims in the Middle East still regard blacks as slaves. It would be worse than blasphemy for them to believe either Allah or Muhammad were black. Most Asians and Arabs despise blacks. As a matter of fact, blacks receive better treatment from white people than from Asians or Middle Easterners. Just live in those societies and experience it for yourselves. Many people in Africa know that Arab countries have not responded to atrocities in places like Darfur and Sudan because the people getting slaughtered there are black Africans.

Muhammad on women.

Muhammad taught that the majority of the people in hell were women. "The prophet said, "I was shown the Hell-fire and that the majority of its dwellers were women" Hadith, Vol. 1, nos. 28,301; Vol.2, no.161. The reason the majority of the people in hell were women is stated in vol.2, no.541. "O women I have not seen anyone more deficient in intelligence and religion than you. Muhammad believed that women were “deficient in intelligence” and thus they should not be given equal rights under Islamic Law. For example, he legislated that a woman’s testimony in court was worth only half that of a man. Thus it would take the testimony of two women to offset the testimony of a man. Imagine what this would do to women who were raped. We have read numerous stories in Muslim countries where rape victims were punished instead of the rapist. “The Prophet said, “Isn’t the witness of a woman equal to half of that of a man” The woman said, yes.” He said, “This is because of the deficiency of a woman’s mind” (Vol.3, no.826) Muhammad even ruled that women are to receive only half of what their brothers receive in inheritance Vol.4, no10. Thus women are financially punished for being females. Perhaps the most degrading picture of women is that paradise will have beautiful women chained in different corners. Women’s only role is to satisfy the sexual urges of men, chain. The statement of Allah, Beautiful women restrained (chains) in pavilions. Allah’s Apostle said, “In paradise there is a pavilion made of a single hollow pearl sixty miles wide and in each corner there are wives who will not see those in the other corners; and the believers will visit and enjoy them”.

No dogs allowed

We have heard scores of stories of Muslim taxi drivers in different cities in America who refused to give a ride for blind passengers with guide dogs. “Angels will not enter a house if a dog is there” according to Vol.4, no.539. Thus Hadith no. 540, vol.4 reads “Allah’s Apostle ordered that the dogs should be killed. If you are a dog lover you cannot be a good Muslim

QURAN

Here's a sample of a dialog between a Muslim and a Non-Muslim:

Muslim: The quran is true in all things.
Non-Muslim: But it contradicts the Biblical Jesus.
Muslim: Then the Bible is corrupt.
Non- Muslim: But how do you know that the Bible is corrupt? Do you have any textual proof?
Muslim: I don't need any textual proof because I know that the Bible is corrupt.
Muslim: Muhammad is the prophet of God.
Non-Muslim: Why is this true?
Muslim: The Quran says so
Non-Muslim: Why is the Quran true?
Muslim: The Quran is without error.
Non-Muslim: Do you have any proof that the Quran is true?
Muslim: The prophet said the Quran is the word of god.

Changes in the Quran

One interesting way some of the original verses of the Quran were lost is that a follower of Muhammad named Abdollah Sarh would make suggestions to Muhammad about rephrasing, adding to, or subtracting from the Suras. Muhammad often did as Sarh suggested. Ali Dashti narrates. "Abdollah renounced Islam on the ground that the revelations, if from God, could not be changed at the prompting of a scribe such as he. After his apostasy he went to Mecca and joined the Qurayshites." It is no wonder that when Muhammad conquered Mecca one of the first people he killed was Abdollah, for he knew too much and opened his mouth too often.

Abrogated Verses

In the abrogation process, verses which are contradictory to Muslim faith and practice have been removed from the text, such as the "Satanic Verses' in which Muhammad approved of the worship of the three goddesses, the daughters of Allah.

Added Verses

Not only have parts of the Quran been lost, but entire verses and chapters have been added to it. For example, Ubai had several Suras in his manuscript of the quran which Uthman omitted from his standardized text. Thus there were Qurans in circulation before Othman's text which had additional revelations from Muhammad which Uthman did not find or approve of, and thus he failed to place them in his text.

Chapter 10

Western Misunderstanding of Islam

Western people have a difficult time comprehending Islam because they fail to understand that it is a form of cultural imperialism in which the religion and culture of seventh – century Arabia have been raised to the status of divine law. The difficulty in understanding Islam is rooted in the traditional western philosophic concept of the secular versus sacred dichotomy. In the West, organized religion is not viewed as having power to rule over all of life; instead, there is a secular realm in which organized religion has no authority. Thus there is a wall of separation between church and state. For example, religious organizations in the West cannot set speed limits or legislate political laws. Islam cannot be viewed simply as one's private or personal religious preference. There is no secular realm in Islamic countries. In Pakistan and other Islamic countries, if someone doesn't like a person, he can concoct a story against him and accuse him of insulting the Prophet or the Quran. Then a mob would come and burn him alive. In Pakistan the mob kills a lot of Christians on fraudulent charges.

Religion in the West is personal and private. For example, Christianity does not demand that people today should dress in accordance with first- century dress codes, or they can eat only what Jesus ate. Christianity is thus supra-cultural in that it allows people to live, dress, and eat in accordance with the culture in which they are living. But this is not so with Islam. Whenever Islam becomes the dominant religion in a country, it alters the culture of that nation and transforms it into the culture of the seventh century Arabia. This is why it is so hard for Muslims to convert to another religion. Every aspect of life has been dictated by Islam. The Muslim must follow the dictates of Islam regardless of where he lives or what he thinks about it. Egyptian born Victor Khalil says "Islam regulates every aspect of life, to the point that culture, religion and politics in a Muslim country are practically inseparable." Muhammad took the Arab culture around him, with all its secular and sacred customs, and made it into the religion of Islam.

Muhammad took the political laws which governed seventh –century Arabian tribes and made them into the laws of Allah. In such tribes the Sheik, or chief, had absolute authority over those under him. There was no concept of civil or personal rights in seventh century Arabia. The head of the tribe decided whether you lived or died. This is why Islamic countries are always inevitably ruled by kings, dictators, or strong men, who rule as despots.

The historical evidence is clear that Muhammad adopted the pagan religious rite of a pilgrimage to Mecca to worship at the Kabah in order to appease the Meccan merchants who made a tremendous amount of money out of these pilgrimages. The pilgrimage has been both cruel and unnecessary and has fostered great hardships upon poor third world Muslims who have had to skimp and save their entire lives in order to fulfill this "pillar' of Islam.

Veil

Arabian tribal women used to wear the veil and Islam adopted this in every nation. Being covered from head to toe to be protected from the desert sun and dust is both practical and understandable if you are living in a desert. Arabian women dressed that way long before Muhammad was born. However, to impose such a desert garb on women everywhere is a form of cultural imperialism. The Quran is the most antinomian religion in the world. Sura 4:34 says men are the managers of the affairs of women. Those whom you fear may be rebellious, admonish; or banish to their couches and beat them. "

Medina Legacy: Jihad against Jews. The Jews of Arabia

In approximately 1400 BC over 2000 years before the first Muslim invasion of Palestine (as the Romans renamed it), Israel was already established as a nation.

A civil war split Israel into two nations during the time of Rehoboam, Solomon's son. The ten tribes of the northern land known as Samaria called themselves Israel. The southern tribes of Judah, Benjamin and Levi became known as the Kingdom of Judah, from which the name "Jew" came.

The Assyrian Dispersion

Israel entered a continuous spiral of apostasy until Jehovah finally sent the Assyrians to destroy them in 721 BC. The survivors of the ten tribes were taken captive into Assyria. Why is this necessary to know? Because some of the survivors of this dispersion fled to Arabia and settled there.

The Babylonian Dispersion

The southern Kingdom of Judah experienced intermittent revivals but finally fell into the same apostasy as the Samarian kingdom. Though Judah was repeatedly warned, they did not listen. 2 Chron.: 36: 15-21, Isaiah 39:5-7) The Babylonian destruction was predicted by Isaiah 150 years before it happened.

The Bible records that not all of the Jews were taken to Babylon. A few were left in Judea by the Babylonians to maintain the land. Some were able to flee to Egypt and others to Arabia.

In 1949, after the birth of the state of Israel, Israelis rescued the Yemenite Jews from the wrath of the Muslims in an operation known as "the wings of Eagles". They were all airlifted to Israel. The Yemenite Jews trace their origins in Arabia back 2500 years, during the time of the Babylonian invasion.

The Roman Dispersion

The greatest flood of Jewish refugees resulted from the initial Roman destruction of Jerusalem and Judea in AD

70, and continued for some 150 years. During this time, the Romans fought off different Jewish Guerilla-style wars that tried to reclaim Jerusalem. Finally, the Jewish resistance was totally crushed. Some survivors stayed on in Israel while others fled. Yathrib or Medina was established by Jews.

The second holiest city in the Islamic world was first established by Jews, an amazing fact confirmed by historical sources.

Mohammad's zealous crusade against polytheism made him increasingly unpopular in his hometown of Mecca. When they tried to kill him, he and his followers fled to Yathrib. Mohammad tried to win the Jews over by representing himself as simply a teacher of the creed of Abraham. He even adopted the Jewish Sabbath, some dietary laws and initially required prayer toward Jerusalem rather than Mecca.

Believe or Be Beheaded

The Jews however were not deceived and refused to acknowledge him as anything but a false prophet. This infuriated Mohammad. To attract Jews, Muhammad had tried to encourage the Jews to accept his prophet hood by preaching monotheism, observing the Jewish Sabbath, praying toward Jerusalem, appealing to Abraham and the Patriarchs, adopting some of their dietary laws and praising their scriptures. But the Jews rejected him.

He turned to what would become his standard pattern: the use of the sword. He marched against this Jewish tribe and besieged their village. When they surrendered and came out one by one, they were beheaded. The first Muslim massacre was executed on the Jews. The pattern of "confess Islam or face sword" was established. He changed the direction of prayer from Jerusalem to Mecca, dropped the Saturday Sabbath and adopted the pagan Friday Sabbath instead. Mohammad was anxious to spread Islam beyond Medina.

The Quraysh model of Meccan conquest

Three years after the battle of Badr, a 10,000 man Meccan army again laid siege to Medina. The Quraysh tribe of Mecca was not able to conquer Medina and Mohammad was not strong enough to defeat them. So Mohammad signed a ten-year treaty of non-aggression with Mecca.

By AD. 630, less than a year later, Mohammad had built up his army. He stormed Mecca by surprise and conquered it, thus making himself ruler of the city of his birth. Mohammad's first act was to establish Mecca as the holiest city of Islam. Mohammad proclaimed the Kabah as "Haram" (forbidden to non-Muslims)

Muslims have quoted the "Quraysh model" as justification for many deceptive treaties. It means "Negotiate Peace with your enemy until you become strong enough to annihilate him". It is called the "Hudna" agreement. This is the justification chairman Yasser Arafat gave to his critics who condemned him for signing the Oslo agreement.

Why Jews were persecuted

Mohammad and his disciples treated the Jews more severely than any other "unbeliever". They had irritated him by their refusal to recognize him as a prophet. Mohammad decided these non-believers in his homeland had to be eliminated if he was going to fulfill his ambitions. So he ordered an Islamic Law. "Two religions may not dwell together on the Arabian Peninsula".

The Arabian Holocaust

After issuing this decree, he started to enforce it immediately. He went after Jewish communities of Northern Arabia, systematically slaughtering them all. First, the Qurazia tribe was exterminated. Then Mohammad sent messengers to the Jewish community at the oasis of Khaibar, "inviting" Usayr, and their war chief, to visit Medina for peace negotiations. Usayr set off with 30 companions and a Muslim escort suspecting no foul play. The Jews went unarmed. On the way the Muslims turned upon the defenseless delegation, killing all but one who managed to escape. Mohammad attacked and destroyed their whole community.

Mohammad justified this treachery saying "war is deception". War practiced according to this Muslim doctrine was not just deception, it was like hell.

The complete annihilation of the two Arabian-Jewish tribes, with every man, woman and child slaughtered is according to the late Israeli historian and President Itzhak Ben-Zvi, "a tragedy for which no parallel can be found in Jewish history".

In the war against Islamic Fundamentalist terrorism, it would be good for Western leaders to remember this "Islamic tactic of warfare ". According to this religious doctrine of Islam, what they say does not have to be true- after all, war is deception; the end justifies the means.

A Heritage of brutality

As an example of their brutality and barbarity, after one Jewish town surrendered to the Muslims, about 1000 men were beheaded in one day. The woman and children were sold into slavery.

Elsewhere, as the attacks on Jews continued, some managed to survive. Under a new Islamic Policy, non-Muslims or "infidels" were permitted to maintain their land so long as they paid as 50 percent tribute for "protection".

Thus the Jewish Dhimmi evolved- the robbery of freedom and political independence compounding the extortion and eventual expropriation of property. Operated between onslaughts, expulsions, and pillages from the Arab Muslim conquest onward, the non-Muslim Dhimmi, predominantly Jewish, but with Christians too- provided the important source of religious revenue through the "infidel's head tax." He became very quickly a convenient political scapegoat and whipping boy as well.

The Precedent of Prey

The betrayal and killing of Jews in Medina, the massacres of the Nadhir and Kainuka tribes and the dispossession of property by Muslims set up what Joan Peters calls:

"The Precedent of Prey"- a pattern that would be repeated again and again. The agrarian and merchant Jews lucky enough to escape death would be plundered and exploited by nomadic Arabs. Islam not only gave them an excuse for such oppression, it commanded it. All over the world today- from Georgia to Azerbaijan to Serbia to India to Sudan and Eritrea, Muslims are killing others.

Hate, a Religious Doctrine

What began as a rivalry between brothers degenerated into a family feud? It evolved into an everlasting, irreconcilable hatred.

There were some cases of reconciliation between the Arabs and the Jews of Arabia in the centuries before the birth of Mohammad. They were not loved, but they were accepted.

Hatred of Jews in Islam is justified as a religious cause. Islam literally resurrected the ancient enmities and jealousies of the sons of Ishmael, Esau and Keturah toward Jews, and enshrined them as religious doctrine.

Deification of 7th century Arab culture

The tribal aspect of pre- Islamic Arabia explains many of the things that can be found in Islam today. For example, it was perfectly in line with Arab morality to mount raids on other tribes in order to obtain wealth, wives, and slaves, and so the tribes were constantly at war with one another. The same behavior pattern is seen now in 2014 and 2015 in Syria and Iraq by ISIS fighters. The desert tribes lived by the code of an eye for an eye and a tooth for a tooth. Vengeance was extracted whenever anything was done to hurt any member of the tribe. It meant nothing to them to cut off the hand, foot or tongue. Even the ears were lopped off and the eyes were gouged out as punishment for various crimes. To sneak up behind someone and slit his throat from ear to ear was viewed as the right thing to do in certain situations, and the person who did it was viewed as a hero. Forcing people into slavery or kidnapping women, holding them in your harem, and raping them at will was considered pleasing to Allah. The harsh Arabian climate produced a harsh tribal society in which violence was the norm, and violence is still an attribute of Islamic societies.

The desperate plight of Salman Rushdie is a modern example. To receive a death sentence for writing a book which gives an unfavorable view of Muhammad is something a Westerner does not understand or tolerate. However, for a Muslim, it makes perfect sense. The Danish cartoonist, Kurt Westergaard, was attacked on January 1. 2010, by a 28-year-old Somali Muslim with an axe. He survived the attack. His crime was drawing a cartoon of the Prophet Muhammad. Theo Van Gogh, a Dutch film maker who made a T.V. film critical of Islam, was shot and stabbed to death on an Amsterdam street in November 2004.

The Muslim religion actually froze in time the seventh century Arab culture of Mecca and raised it to the level of being a “Divine Revelation”- how all people should live for all time. The modern concept of “Jihad” primarily has to do with forcing this culture upon the world- either by conversion or by conquest.

In a profound, almost mystical sense, Mohammed is the product of the seventh century Arab culture and the Muslim religion is an expression of his perceptions of it; a major part of this being revulsion of the Jews. Mohammad never forgave them for rejecting him and his claim of being God's Prophet. That hostility was woven into the Quran.

Religions- cultural imperialism

Islam is nothing less than a religious –cultural imperialism that works to take over the world. This is why Mohammad divided the earth into two spheres.

1. Dar al-Islam –the land of peace
2. Dar-al- Harb – the land of war.

Mohammad believed the Muslim is in a perpetual state of "Jihad"- holy war" – with all countries in the Dar-al-Harb sphere. The true follower believes that Allah has willed for Muslims to establish Islamic ways over the whole world – either by conversion or by sword.

Islam believes this doctrine is especially applicable to the Middle East, which they claim as the center of their world.

Israel's victories over the armies of Allah in five wars have placed the Quran in jeopardy, for it promises the forces of Islam victory in holy wars.

Chapter 11

The Untold Refugee Story

If you read about the Middle East problem in the newspaper or listen to the discussions in the news, you can't help but be bombarded by analysts suggesting the key to peace is resolving "the Palestinian refugee issue". There is another untold side of the Middle East refugee story.

The world seldom hears about a million refugees who fled Arab terror and hatred and settled in Israel.
Why the cover up?

Why isn't this story reported? Why isn't it chronicled? Why isn't it remembered? If Arab nations are responsible for expelling Jews in the same numbers as was the much publicized Arab refugees displaced after the creation of Israel, why isn't the obvious solution a simple population exchange? The enormity of the Muslim myth being swallowed by the West is nowhere more graphically illustrated than in this issue. There is no moral equivalence in this situation. The Jews did not drive out Palestinian refugees. They were not threatened or killed so as to terrorize survivors into leaving.

In many cases Palestinians were begged to stay. However, they were ordered to leave "temporarily" by the combined Muslim armies who promised to annihilate Jews and the new state.

On the other hand, Jews living in Arab countries were terrorized, murdered and driven out. Their properties and assets were confiscated. Those who escaped were thankful just to be left alone. The Jews were received and immediately repatriated into the new fragile state of Israel. They were given aid and jobs to the best ability of the struggling new country.

The Palestinians were deliberately forced into refugee camps and not permitted to integrate into the society of their unwilling hosts, even though they were fellow Muslims. They didn't even try to help them; instead they prevailed upon the UNO to supply the refugees' needs. Kept in these camps by their own people for more than 67 years, they are used as political pawns so that Muslim negotiations can continue to trump up charges of "Israeli aggression."

Some popular Muslims mythology

Many myths have been spun to suppress the facts about Jewish immigration from Arab lands. Let us review some of the tales that teach the exact opposite of the truth.

Myth #1: The Arabs have nothing against Jews in general and lived in peace and harmony with them, until the creation of the Zionist movement and consequent creation of the state of Israel in 1948.

Myth #2: Alienation of Jews began in large part because Israel is almost entirely made up of European Jews who displaced indigenous Arab peoples in Palestine.

Myth # 3: The Key to resolving the Middle East crisis is to stop Israeli aggression and occupation of Arab lands and to create an independent Palestinian State.

Myth # 4: Israel's US supplied military weapons have been practiced against the peaceful neighbors.

These myths have worked like magic for Muslim propagandists for decades, but especially for all negotiations. You hear the propaganda "Israeli aggression and occupation of Arab Land. The real truth is that half of the Jewish population of Israel are refugees or offspring of refugees from Arab countries.

Collective Amnesia

For some reason, the whole world has swallowed unbelievable products of the Arab propaganda machine. The fact that the Zionist struggle was active mainly in Europe and America and the fact that ignorance has prevailed concerning the Dhimmi condition and its aftereffects (insecurity, fear and silence) have led to Zionism's being viewed as an exclusively Western movement.

An incredible Irony:

Modern media invented a perfect term for what Muslim nations have done with the history of "Dhimmis"- Turn-speak which means "a cynical inverting or distorting of facts, which for example, makes the victim appear to be the oppressor. Arab propagandists have used turns to speak perfectly in perpetuating the myth of "displaced" and "terrorized" Arabs in the Jewish settled area of Palestine-cum- Israel.

The record shows that migrant Muslims came from other Arab countries to areas of Palestine that were re-claimed and developed by Jews in order to get jobs. It was afterward that they began to claim Jews displaced them from land that had been in their families for hundreds of years.

There have been colossal injustices inflicted on the people of Palestine- only it wasn't Jews who committed the injustices but Muslims-who sought to drive Jews out of a plot of land that was only a fraction of what was originally mandated to them by the League of Nations. When the map of the Middle East was completely redrawn after the fall of the Turkish Ottoman Empire in 1917, Arab States were created from the stateless remains of the Ottoman occupation and a certain section was mandated to the Jews as a homeland. No matter how small the Jewish state was made, it was still too big for Muslims-because it isn't the size of Israel that matters to Muslims, it is the existence of Israel.

The Rule of Hatred

The most cynical myth of all, however, is the lie that Jews enjoyed freedom, liberty and kind treatment while dwelling in Muslim ruled lands before the rise of Zionism. Here are some impartial observations of the Jews or Dhimmi's treatment.

In their Holy Land, the Jews as well as Christians suffered long from harsh discrimination. According to the British consulate report in 1839, the Jewish life was not much above that of a dog.

In truth, "Arab" terrorism in the Holy Land originated centuries before the recent toll of the Palestinian cause was invented. In towns where Jews lived for hundreds of years, those Jews were periodically robbed, raped in some places, massacred, and in many instances, the survivors were obliged to abandon their possessions and run.

In the early seventeenth century, a pair of Christian visitors to Galilee told of life for the Jews "Life here is the poorest and most miserable that one can imagine. Because of the harshness of Turkish rule and its crippling Dhimmi oppression, the Jews pay for the very air they breathe". The monstrous myth, that there was no problem for the Jews living peacefully with the Muslims until the rise of Zionism and the founding of the state of Israel, is a classic example of Muslim Turn-speak and the cynical hatred motivating it.

A technique of propaganda called "Turn-speak": The Arab league makes use of a cognitive technique of propaganda called "Turn-speak", where you attack someone and then turn it around 180 degrees and claim they attacked you. Because the truth is the exact opposite of the information being disseminated, it is psychologically difficult to counter and leads to confusion.

The term was first used by journalists to describe German propaganda after it invaded Czechoslovakia in March of 1939. To win sympathy for their invasion, the Germans practiced what has become known as "Turn-speak". They turned the blame back on the Czechs for trying to precipitate in an all-out war in the region. In other words, the (Czechs in their attempt to hang on to their land were ready to plunge all of Europe into war.) How did the rest of Europe respond to this lie? They believed it. World leaders decided that something had to be done to preserve peace at any cost.

From the crusades to the Ottoman Turk Empire: The last European Crusade

The eighth and final European crusade was led by the King of France. It ended in A.D 1291 with the fall of the last Christian stronghold in the Holy Land- the port city of Acre (Akko in Hebrew). There would not be another European attempt to liberate the Holy Land for 500 years. Oddly enough another French King, Napoleon Bonaparte, would launch it. He arrived in 1798. Interestingly, Napoleon's quest failed because he suffered his first military defeat at Acre.

By God's providence, Napoleon's cannons were captured while being transported from Alexandria to Joppa when British Admiral Nelson intercepted and defeated the French Navy. Napoleon arrived and was bombarded by his own artillery. Some of his best and bravest soldiers were lost before he gave up and left.

God's hand was in this; for Napoleon had promised his Jewish financiers he would capture the Holy Land and establish the State of Israel. This would have been out of God's predicted timetable; Hebrew prophets prophesied God would bring back the scattered sons of Israel and cause the nation to be born shortly before the coming of the Messiah.

The Mongol Invasion of Muslims

The Mongol tribes were united under Chief Temujin in A.D 1206. He was renamed Genghis Khan, which meant "super ruler". He charged across the steppes and over the Caucuses Mountains to take on the Muslim empire. The formidable Mongol cavalry and fierce warriors were virtually unstoppable. By A.D 1258, the goddess horde, led by Genghis Khan's grandson Hulague Khan, destroyed the Abbasid Caliphate of Baghdad as well as the Seljuk sultanate in Asia Minor.

The Mongols posed a tremendous threat to Asia, the Middle East and Europe. They were finally defeated by Muslim Mamelukes at the battle of Ain Jalut in A.D 1260.

Origin of the Ottoman Empire

After the Mongols had passed, a young Turkish mercenary named Othman, he gathered some of the shattered Seljuk's forces together and began to impose order amid ruin. Othman slowly extended his martial Law through Asia Minor. After many years of struggle, he created the only kind of state feasible amid wreckage left by the Mongols. It was a military dictatorship of which he became the first sultan. (Asia Minor –Turkey). In A.D 1288, Uthman, the first Sultan of all Turks, formed the Uthman Muslim Dynasty. It soon became known by its variant name – the Ottoman Empire. Their leaders were called Sultans instead of Caliphs.

For the next six centuries, 37 descendants of the house of Uthman or Othman ruled the empire. It became one of the largest and richest in history.

The Ottoman Empire affected on the Middle East

The Ottoman Turks were not, and never considered themselves to be a part of the Arab world.

To Arabs as to Europeans, the Ottoman Turks were essentially foreign masters. They literally obliterated the State identities and boundaries of the Middle East. For the next four centuries, there were no nation- states such as Syria, Lebanon, Iraq/Babylon, Arabia, Persia etc. They were simply territories ruled by Ottoman Viziers from major cities.

Palestine, for instance, included what are now known as Syria, Lebanon, Jordan and Israel and was ruled from Damascus. There were no independent Arab nations and no defined boundaries.

When the British liberated the area from the Ottoman Turks, no Arab had any more valid claim to a specific land or state than the Jew did. As a matter of fact, the Jews had a mandate of specific land ratified by the League of Nations. Not one Arab State could claim this kind of ratification from such a world authority.

The Palestinians from Bosnia- Herzegovina

To counteract the effect of some Jewish emigration that took place between 1847 and 1880, Ottoman authorities began an affirmative action program to resettle European Muslims in Palestine. While Arabs often make much of the European Heritage of many of Israel's Jews, calling them "foreign invaders", the truth is, many of today's so-called Palestinians have European roots going back only a generation or two.

During the latter stages of the receding Ottoman Empire, beginning around 1878, Muslim refugees from the lost Islamic Provinces of Europe streamed into Palestine

The Ottoman government settled these immigrants in troubled regions, thereby tightening its control through a policy of Muslim colonization. In 1878, after annexation of Bosnia- Herzegovina by Austria, Bosnian Muslim colonists arrived in Macedonia and on the coastal plains of Palestine

.

Ottoman Desolation of Holy Land

The Holy Land under the Ottoman Turks suffered more devastation in four hundred years than the previous fifteen hundred. By the 19th century, the ancient canal and irrigation systems were destroyed. The land was barren and filled with Malaria ridden swamps. The hills were denuded of trees and brush so all of the terraces and top soil had eroded away, leaving only rocks.

The Curse of the Turk "Effendis"

With the horrible condition of the land in the late 19th century, most Muslim inhabitants of the Holy Land were eager to leave if a buyer for their property could be found.

The amazing Jewish reclamation

From the 1880's through 1918, Jews returning to Palestine faced a harsh life in a barren malaria-infested land. Still they came and by the turn of the century, Jewish villages dotted the countryside. A few years later, Jews represented a majority of the population in Jerusalem. There was new life in

Haifa, Safed and Tiberius. In 1909, the first modern all-Hebrew city was founded on the sands of the Mediterranean –Tel Aviv.

Far from being run off the land, the Muslim population benefited greatly from these developments. Quickly, opportunities arose for three Arab groups.

1. The landless population looking for work.
2. The people indebted to the absentee landlords
3. The Effendis themselves, who sold land to the Jews at astronomical prices.

The "Effendis" sowed the seeds of the Middle East Crisis

The Effendis collected taxes for the Turkish administration and controlled the populace from their seats on governing councils. However, before long, many of them saw their little feudal empires threatened by the growing influence of the Jews. So they resorted to the age-old tactic that always worked in Muslim history- make the Jews scapegoats.

Effect of World War I on Palestine
How the British set up the Middle East Crisis?

The British were to receive a lesson from the age-old Arab Adage: "Promise an Arab a centimeter and he will demand a Kilometer". Another gross British misunderstanding was with the Muslim religious power structure. The sheriff of Mecca did not have the same authority and control over Islam as the Pope does over the Roman Catholic Church. Yet this was the basic assumption on which their planned control of the Arabs depended. The

Turks had destroyed the Arab Caliphate in Mecca centuries before. So the Arabs had no controlling authority with which to deal. There was only a horde of warring tribes wanting to get the best deal in the great land grab following the collapse of the Ottoman Empire.

Britain's' first step in achieving its glorious imperial ambition was to enlist Arabs in their fight against the Turks. The first contact was with Hussein Ibn -Ali, Sheriff of Mecca. Hussein was promised much of Arabia and vast amounts of gold and arms if he led a revolt against the Turks. A key player was Lt. Col. T.E Lawrence of Arabia.

England awakens to Bible Prophesy

To fully appreciate the miracle of Israel's rebirth in the modern world, the motivation of its on-again off-again sponsor, England, requires examination. England had a long fascination with the Holy Land dating back to its earliest days of Christianity. In 1948, the Jewish state was reborn, due in large measure to the spiritual vision of British students of prophecy. The large Prophecy conferences influenced the whole nation, even members of Parliament.

Many camp meetings were set up annually to pursue and learn about Bible Prophecy. Such articulate luminaries in this movement as John Nelson Darby, William Kelly and Sir Robert Anderson spoke to large crowds about the sudden coming of Jesus Christ for his Church. They also lined the return of Jews to the Holy Land as an indispensable part of the final scenario. They not only believed in a literal rebirth of the state of Israel, but also insisted that God's purpose for the Jews as a people and a nation, which was promised throughout the Old Testament, would be fulfilled.

England took up the cause of restoring Israel once more in the early twentieth century. However, Lord Balfour's declaration would not have been possible without the strong biblical case made for Israel by the British Bible Prophecy studies conducted at Powers Court Castle in the 19th century.

Benjamin Disraeli, who would rise to become Prime Minister, was one of the most provocative figures in British history. A Jewish convert to Christianity, he was more concerned with the world's debt to the Jews than the Jews' future in the world. In 1878, Disraeli recaptured Cyprus for Britain and purchased Suez, both geographically speaking, a mere stone's throw from the Holy Land. Disraeli knew it was just a matter of time.

Lord Balfour

The next British leader to pursue the vision was Arthur James Balfour, who, as England's foreign minister, signed the famous Balfour Declaration mandating the recreation of the Jewish state. He too, believed religion, and civilization in general, owed Judaism an immeasurable debt, shamefully ill repaid."

Britain's Betrayal: The sellout of the Jews

Of all the injustices perpetuated against the Jewish people in the Holy Land, the worst was how their country has been continually reduced from its original mandated size. There has continually been a sizable Jewish remnant living in the Holy Land, despite the Roman destruction in AD 70 and the crushing of Jewish rebellions in the second century AD. In the 18th and 19th centuries, Jews outnumbered Muslims in Jerusalem. During the four centuries under Ottoman Turkish control, the Holy Land reached its ultimate state of desolation. The absentee landlords, known as Effendis, practiced such callous usury and taxation on the poor Arab farmers that they were eventually overwhelmed with debt and fled the land.

Whence cometh the Palestinians

There was no Palestinian state or people known as "Palestinians". The few Arabic-speaking people living there considered themselves "Ottomans", Turks, Southern Syrians, or simply Arab People but never Palestinians. The migratory Bedouins who seasonally moved through the area never laid claim to the land. The Jews, who began returning to the Holy land throughout the mid-nineteenth century bought land from the all-too-willing–to sell Effendis for enormously inflated prices.

With the price of Herculean labor and the loss of many lives to malaria, the Jews began to reclaim the land and make it flourish. This development encouraged a significant number of poor Arab-Muslims to flock there in order to find work and a better standard of living. Jews became victims of their own success. Little did they realize the very ones they were helping, would turn and claim the Jews had stolen their land that had belonged to Arab families for hundreds of years?

The Balfour Declaration

Because of the existing conditions in the Middle East, Lord Balfour and other members of the British Parliament thought that setting forth the propositions contained in the Balfour declaration was not an invasion of Arab-Muslim land. The motto of the forming committee was "A people for a land, for a land without a people". Furthermore, the League of Nations concurred with the "Declaration" for the same reasons.

The League of Nations Mandate

The boundaries of the new nation were defined and approved unanimously by the League of Nations three years after the Balfour Declaration. Britain was given authority over the entire Middle East from the Mediterranean to the borders of India.

The territory to become the state of Israel, then variously referred to as "Palestine" "Western Palestine" South Syria or even as part of Turkey, extended east and west of the Jordan River from the Mediterranean to Arabia and Iraq, and North and South from Egypt to Lebanon and Syria. On present day maps, that includes most of Jordan, Southern Lebanon and the Sinai.

Simultaneously, independent Arab statehood was being granted in Syria, Iraq and Saudi Arabia. Arab leaders were initially satisfied with their acquisition and didn't question the status of Jewish Palestine.

Britain gives away 75 percent of the Jewish Mandated Land

It was not long, however, before Abdullah, brother of Faisal Ibn Hussein, decided he should have Trans Jordan as his kingdom. He protested to the British who unilaterally decided to carve out of Jewish Palestine 75 percent of its mandated land, then known as the Trans Jordan and hand it over to Abdullah.

It should be explained why Abdullah, who was a Hashemite, was in Trans Jordan: The tribe of Ibn Saud and his fanatical sect of Wahhabi Muslims had just driven the Hashemite Tribe out of Mecca and Medina, taking over the holy sites and all of Arabia.

The Hashemite had been custodians of Mecca and Medina for centuries. Faisal, the ruler of the Hashemites, was the one with whom the British Foreign Office made promises to, for fighting against the Turks. Abdullah argued the British gave his brother Faisal ibn Hussein both Syria and Iraq, but gave him nothing. The British foreign office quietly scrambled to offer him the major part of land they were bound by the League of Nations mandate to give Israel.

Transjordan became the Arab country comprising 38000 square miles. When Israel came into existence in 1948 it only got less than 8000 square miles. 35000 square miles of the Jewish National Homeland were given to Arabs. Thus 80% of their mandated land was lost to the Jews.

Britain violated its mandate

When Britain gave Transjordan to Abdullah, it specifically violated article 5 of the mandate giving

unanimous approval by the League of Nations at the San Remo conference on July 24, 1922.
Today the actual Palestine is the country of Jordan

References

"God's War on Terror" by Walid Shoebat with Joel Richardson
"The sword of the prophet" by serge Trifkovic
"Islam prophesied in Genesis" by Dennis Avi Lipkin
"Answering Islam" by Norman Geisler and Abdal Saleeb
"Return to Mecca" by Dennis Avi Lipkin

Chapter 12

Arguments for Islam and the Answers

It is very important for the Christian Church to know the challenge of Islam and how to respond to it. There are 7 to 9 million Muslims living in America. Many Christians interact with Muslims every day, as co-workers and neighbors. Thus, it is very important for every Christian to have a better understanding of Islam, what Muslims believe and how to respond to the typical Muslim's questions about the Christian faith.

It is also important not to stereotype Islam as a simple religion that promotes violence. In fact, Islam had a rich tradition in its intellectual history and in its cultural achievements. Throughout history, the Muslim world has produced many philosophers and scientists.

There is a fundamental difference between Islam and Christianity in four main areas. 1) The nature and the authority of the Bible. (2) The nature of God 3) the view of human kind 4) the view of Christ. Islam and Christianity have diametrically opposed ideas on these four important points.

The theological challenges that Islam presents to the Christian faith are not only from Muslims. Western intellectuals, liberals, Christian scholars, and the so called enlightenment thinkers have expressed basically the very same challenges to Christianity that Muslims have expressed for the past 1400 years. It is, therefore, understandable that Muslims feel intellectually justified in rejecting Christianity. They might say "we have been saying these things against Christianity for 1400 years and now your own Western scholars and your Christian writers are saying these same things that we have been saying all along."

Immanuel Kant and Thomas Jefferson expressed their doubts about the doctrine of the Trinity. According to many Christian scholars the doctrine of the Trinity is incomprehensible. A Muslim might say "Our holy book, the Quran, told us 1400 years ago that there is only one God and we should worship that God; and that Christians have been misled from the teachings of the Prophet Jesus when they have professed the doctrine of the Trinity.

Another fundamental conviction of the Christian faith is that we are born in a state of sin, that Adam's sin has affected us. However, many surveys indicate that the vast majority of Americans, including evangelical Christians, believe that we are basically good people. A Muslim might respond by saying "we have been saying for all these years that human kind is basically good and now Western people, including Christians are coming to the same conclusions."

Also, the Christian faith believes that it is only because of Jesus' death on the cross that we can have any hope of salvation, our sins have been imputed to Him and His righteousness has been imputed to us. Islam, on the other hand, claims that all people are responsible for their own actions and for their own salvation. Nobody else can pay for someone else's sins.

The idea that God forgives human sin by virtue of punishing an innocent figure in our place raises a host of moral difficulties. Many Christians even view individuals as morally autonomous agents: I am responsible only for my own choices. Such a moral perspective poses many questions for the theory of atonement. How can the suffering of an innocent person take away my guilt?

Islam has a great appeal to people of all backgrounds because it presents itself as a very rational, intellectual, and easy to understand faith. Muslims believe Christianity is filled with mysteries and mumbo jumbo that nobody can understand. People simply have to take all of it by faith. However, Islam presents itself as a very rational simple religion, the religion of nature that any child can understand.

Chapter 13

Islam and Christianity on scripture

The Muslim viewpoint on scripture is this: Because man is prone to being led astray, God has sent prophets throughout history and these prophets have brought revelations from God. According to Islamic belief, all revelations from God prior to the Quran have been either lost or tampered with and corrupted. Thus they are no longer authentic or reliable and therefore no longer authoritative.

The Quran, according to Muslims, is God's final word to humanity and is the only authentic authoritative and reliable information from God, because it is the only information that has not been tampered with and corrupted.

The Quran has many complimentary things to say about the Bible. Sura 5:44 Sura 5:68 Sura 10:94 Sura 29:46

Muhammed very much wanted to say to the Jews and Christians "Listen, I am a monotheist. I am a prophet like Moses and Jesus. We are all alike. We worship the same God. My Quran is basically in confirmation of the previous scriptures. We all agree on the essentials. The Quran is the final word from God but the Law and the Gospel were also guidance, light, revelation, and mercy from God to humanity.

However, since Mohammed himself was not very well educated, he did not have firsthand knowledge about the Christian and the Jewish scriptures. Later, in Islamic history, as Muslims came into contact with Jewish and Christian communities and began to read the Bible, they realized that the Old and New Testaments contradict the Quran on very serious issues.

So Muslims had to come up with a theory to explain this situation. On the one hand, the Quran says that the previous scriptures were the word of God and according to the Quran, "No one can change the word of God." On the other hand, the scriptures from the Christians and Jews do not agree with the teachings of the Quran. What is the solution? The doctrine of "tariff" the Arabic word for corruption claims that the Jews and Christians have corrupted their scriptures and that is why the Bible no longer agrees with the teachings of the Quran.

Some Muslims also say, "Your own scholars say the same thing: that Moses did not write the Torah, that Jesus did not say these things. These were all fabricated and put in the mouths of people like Christ and other folks".

The Fatherhood of God

Another of the most important concepts in the Christian faith is the fatherhood of God. Jesus taught us in the Lord's Prayer to address God as "Our Father in Heaven" [Matt 6:9] We Christians feel privileged to be able to talk to God in such intimate terms. We believe that through faith in Christ we can become adopted children of God. When Christians talk about this to Muslims, they think that they are sharing good news. Christians don't understand that to Muslim ears, that sounds like horrible blasphemy to think of God as our Father and us as His children. To Muslim ears, that sounds like horrible news. To them it sounds blasphemous to think of God as our Father and us as his children. For Quran, to talk about God as our Father implies sexual relations and attributes something that is not right to God: "To him (Allah) is due the primal origin of the heavens and the earth: How can he have a son when he hath no consort? He created all things and he hath full knowledge of all things. (Sura 6:101) It is a blasphemy to say that Allah begets sons like a man or an animal."

However, Christians are not attributing a sexual act to God when we talk about the fatherhood of God or that we are sons of God, but that's not how a Muslim understands it.

The idea of God sexually interacting with human beings is utterly foreign to Judeo-Christian teaching. Obviously when Christianity speaks of the fatherhood of God, the Son of God and the children of God, it does not mean to communicate this idea of physical, biological propagation.

We need to look carefully at how the Old Testament and the New Testament articulate their understanding of the fatherhood of God and the so- called brotherhood of man. Nowhere have we seen a Jewish person addressing God as his father. In Jesus' day, his calling God "Father" was a radical departure from Jewish tradition. Further, in the New Testament that relationship is seen from the other perspective. God is heard speaking from heaven declaring "This is my beloved Son in whom I am well pleased "(Mathew: 17:5)

Jesus also bears the title "Son of God", although in a very carefully guarded way. When Christ is called the Son of God, He is called the monogenesis-the only begotten of the Father. The Church understood very early that this did not mean He had a beginning in time. There wasn't any idea of the Father's procreating in time.

When the Bible speaks in terms of sonship, it refers not only to biological generation: it also speaks regularly of sonship as a description of a relationship of obedience. When Jesus talked about setting people free, the Pharisees became upset, saying "We are Abraham's descendants and have never been in bondage to anyone (John 8:33). Jesus replies "If you were Abraham's children, you would do the works of Abraham". V: 39] To be called a child of God meant one who obeyed God. Son- ship here was defined not in biological terms, but in ethical terms. And in that sense the New Testament speaks of Christ's unique relationship as the One who is perfectly obedient to the Father. Jesus then tells his disciples to pray: "Our Father in heaven" (Matt 6:9). That was radical; that was astonishing initially to those who heard it. Orthodox Jews and Muslims would also be offended because it was a serious departure from their tradition. In fact, from the Fall throughout the Old Testament, there is a history of the wall separating humankind from God because of sin. An angel with a flaming sword guarded the entrance to paradise (Gen 3:24) to prevent us from having an intimate relationship with God.

In Romans 8, Paul writes about the concept of our adoption by God the Father by virtue of the work of the Holy Spirit, who gives us now, as we are adopted into the family of God, the right and the authority to say "Abba Father". (V15). We now have the right to address God as Father; even though we are not His children by nature, we are His children by adoption; by virtue of our relationship with Christ, we are now included in the family of God.

One of the most moving stories in the Old Testament is the story of Jonathan's son Mephibosheth, who was lame in both legs. (2 Samuel 9) When the news came that Saul and Jonathan had been killed, some men in David's camp wanted to kill all of the survivors from Saul's family, lest any would try to seize power from David and keep him from rising to kingship. David was upset about the proposed purge. He asked if there was anybody left from the house of Saul so that he could honor him in memory of his love for Jonathan. David's men found Jonathan's lame son, who had been secreted away and brought him to David. Mephibosheth was terrified. He assumed that he was being delivered for execution; Instead David said that as long as Mephibosheth was alive, he would eat at the king's table and would be regarded as a member of the king's family. This is what happens when we come to the Lord's Table; we come as God's children. Because of the love of the Father for the Son, and our adoption, we can have this filial relationship.

This relationship differs markedly from any found in Islam. {I John 3:1}. Even the apostles in the first century were overwhelmed with amazement that the status of a filial relationship with God would be accorded to us because of the work of Christ.

As we talk with Muslims about the Fatherhood of God, it is important to know and emphasize the fact that we are not talking about physical procreation on the part of God. An emphasis on the aspect of obedience as a definition of sonship is very important.

Trinity

Another major stumbling block Muslims have regarding Christians' view of God has to do with the Trinity.

Muslims believe that the essence of knowledge is the fact that there is one God and one God alone. Islam believes that, theirs is the final religion of God to humanity, and the gift of Islam is to restore pure monotheism to the world. Muslims believe Christianity has been profoundly corrupted by the notion of the Trinity.

Mohammad profoundly misunderstood the Christian doctrine of the Trinity. The early Muslims thought of the Trinity as the Father, Mary, and Jesus. According to Muslims, the doctrine of the Trinity is an incoherent, illogical notion that many Christians themselves don't understand and often cannot explain or defend to an outsider; only Christianity understands the doctrine of the Trinity as affirming monotheism. Christians believe in the Trinity, not as a rational invention of the human mind, but as a revelation of Jesus Christ and Christ was trustworthy as He was the Truth.

The very word Trinity is a combination of "tri" and "unity" and the accent is on the unity; trinity is not tri-theism. Christianity has resisted any heretical idea that there are three parts to God, that there are three beings or three gods in any polytheistic way. The doctrine of the Trinity is often called a contradiction. What is a contradiction? If I say that something is what it is and is not what it is at the same time and in the same relationship, I would be guilty of violating the law of non-contradiction.

The classical definition of contradiction, by the philosopher Aristotle in his system of logic, which he called the "organon" of all science, the necessary instrument for all meaningful discourse, was this: Something cannot be what it is and not be what is at the same time and in the same relationship. The shorthand for that is "A cannot be A and non A at the same and in the same relationship." For example, I can be a Father (A) and a Son (B) at the same time, but not in the same relationship.

A Paradox, on the other hand, is not a contradiction. The "dox" in a paradox comes from the Greek 'dokeo' which means "to seem, to think, or to appear". "Docetism" comes from the same root. The heretical Docetists denied that Jesus had a true body. They said that he was a phantom; He only seemed to be human. Para means "alongside"; thus paradox means that something seems like something else when placed alongside it. A paradox is not a contradiction. It is an apparent contradiction; when you look at it more closely and give it the benefit of the second glance, you can see that, in fact, the terms are not really contradictory.

A paradox may be jarring to the ear. Paul said that I have to become a slave in order to be free (Rom: 6:15-23). That sounds contradictory, but when we examine it, we see that he means I have to be a slave in one sense in order to be free in another sense.

Otherwise, he would be talking nonsense. He is using a paradox, a perfectly legitimate literary form used frequently in many religions and philosophies.

The third category, mystery, is the one that most often is confused with contradiction. In many courses on Christian theology, the first lecture is on the incomprehensibility of God. This does not mean that God is completely unknowable, rather that no human has an exhaustive, categorical understanding of the mind of God: we cannot know God in His exhaustive fullness. Mohammad would agree with that: God has revealed himself to a degree that we can understand, but there are also dimensions of God that are beyond our human understanding. God is infinite in this perspective, but we can never have an infinite perspective of anything because we are finite. An infinite perspective is beyond our ability. This is axiomatic in Islam, in Jewish theology, and in Christian theology.

The church historically has been very careful in setting forth this definition of the Trinity; God is one in essence, three in person. God is one single being but three persons.

He is one in A, but three in B. The plurality is in a different category from the category of being. The church speaks of three "substances" within God, not three distinct essences.

No one can demonstrate that the formula for the Trinity breaks the law of non-contradiction. The doctrine of the Trinity is neither irrational, nor nonsensical, nor contradictory. Christians are monotheists with respect to the essential being of God Himself, but at the same time, we are saying, within the being of God, there are three distinct personae.

However, these personae do not differ from each other in essence, so it is not a distinction in essence. We distinguish within God, even as the Muslims and the Jew do, the various attributes of God: that God is eternal and God is immutable. That does not mean that there are two different parts of God, one being immutable and the other being eternal. Rather, God is immutably eternal and eternally immutable.

The doctrine of Trinity is based on the New Testament teaching on the nature of Christ.

Islam and Christianity on Sin

According to the Quran, there is a master-servant relationship between God and man. God created Adam and Eve, and they sinned. They repented. God forgave them. Basically, the whole history of salvation according to the Quran is that God has sent prophets throughout history to all people groups to guide them to the straight path, the straight path of worshipping one God, doing good deeds, looking forward to the Day of Judgment and living in the light of the Day of Judgment.

The Quran contains several accounts of the creation story, which on the surface seem similar to the biblical account in Genesis. In Sura 2, God creates Adam and Eve which (Sura 2: 35-37) contains this account.

They disobeyed God and God expelled them from Paradise. When they were expelled, God forgave them. Adam, in fact, became the first prophet. According to Islamic theology, Prophets are kept from fundamental or major sins, because they must be purer than the rest of us to be the conduits for receiving God's revelation. Islamic theology has no room for any doctrine of the fall of man. Adam sinned and God forgave him. That is the end of the Story. Adam's sin had no consequence for people who came after Adam. Muslims view Adam's expulsion from Eden as the occasion for the "Rise of man."

Islam believes that human kind is not sinful by nature. The Quran does use such terms as 'ignorant' 'weak-willed', 'arrogant', easily led astray, and ungrateful, to describe human nature.

Islam teaches that people are born innocent and remain so until each makes him or herself guilty by misdeeds. Islam does not believe in original sin; and its scripture interprets Adam's disobedience as his own personal misdeed, a misdeed for which he repented and which God forgave. In this understanding, we have no bad news to tell Muslims, that they are sinners and need salvation; therefore, there is no room for telling them good news later on.

Regarding the doctrine of man, Islam finds itself much in agreement with many people in the West today. Ads for the US Army used the slogan, "Be all that you can be". Muslims say that Christianity makes man a weak creature that is fallen and in desperate need of help, but Islam gives him dignity. It says "Rise Up! You are morally capable of fulfilling God's will for yourself. You can do it! You can take actions for yourself and your neighborhood and clean up your society! That is another significant point of difference between the Christian and Islamic understanding of humankind.

Contemporary Muslim critics of Christianity maintain that they have great allies in their debates from not only Enlightenment thinkers and Western philosophers, but also Christian theologians who support their contentions. The majority of the evangelical Christians believe that human kind is basically good. In the history of Christianity, there are basically only three subdivisions of theology. The Pelagian School, the semi-pelagian school and the Augustinian school. Throughout history the church had to deal with heretics.

For centuries, advocates of semi-pelagianism and of Augustinianism have struggled with each other theologically. Both semi-pelagianism and Augustinianism believe in original sin; the debate is over the extent of the original sin. However, Pelagianism, which was condemned as heretical early on in church history, denies original sin.

Pelagians take the position that Adam's sin affected Adam and only Adam, that sin did not have the power to distort, in anyway, the nature of humankind. That is basically the Muslim view as well.

Thus, before Mohammad, there were Pelagians, teaching this same idea and objecting to the doctrine of original sin. This theology was resurrected in the sixteenth century in the Socianian heresy, which also denied original sin. It was resurrected again in the 19th century by Charles

Finney, who was a charismatic, yet denied any transfer of guilt from Adam to his descendants. There are also many within the neo-liberal and radical left schools who profess to be Christian yet deny the fall of man and original sin.

Even if the Bible didn't teach a doctrine of original sin, natural reason would require it in order to explain the universality of human corruption. If all people were born innocent, and without any bent or inclination towards sin or wickedness, why then do we have the almost universal recognition that nobody is perfect, that everybody sins?

Even humanists will admit that we are not perfect. The universality of corruption is evidence that there is something wrong with the very moral fabric of human nature. Muslims respond to that by saying", People are born innocent and it is society that corrupts them".

How did society get corrupted in the first place? Societies are composed of individuals, and if mankind is basically good, one would assume that at least some societies would be without corruption.

However, we must examine ourselves in light of the ultimate standard of righteousness, which is God's character as presented in the Bible. God calls us to be perfect and holy even as He is holy (I Peter: 1:16)

Paul, writing to the Corinthians, makes this observation: "But they measuring themselves by themselves and comparing themselves among themselves are not wise. (2 Corinthians 10:12). If I compare myself with other people, as long as I can find someone whose wickedness seems to be more heinous and egregious than my own, I can easily flatter myself into thinking that somehow I have arrived at an acceptable state of righteousness in the sight of God.

However, the minute we lift our gaze to God Himself and examine ourselves from the vertical standard of His righteousness, we suddenly see our own sinfulness. This is what happened to Isaiah when he saw a glimpse of the holiness of God and was undone (Isaiah 6:), to Habakkuk when he trembled before the manifestation of the holiness of God (Hab. 3:16; to Job 42:1-6) and to the disciples when they realized the full purity of the Christ with whom they were dealing e.g.: Luke 5:8; John 6:"69) All of a sudden, by contrast, they saw their sinfulness. When we fail to do this, we can falsely conclude that we live in a safe haven of righteousness where there really is not any need for salvation and atonement. There is no need for redemption because there is nothing to be redeemed from.

In the Quran, God is portrayed in highly majestic and sovereign terms: however, in the entire Quran, the word holy is attributed to God only twice. In one verse in Isaiah," Holy, Holy, Holy" (Isa 6:3), there are more references to the holiness of God than in the entire Islamic scripture. This has shaped the limited Muslim understanding of the holiness of God. Further, orthodox Muslims do not believe that God has revealed his will and his commands. However, that will and those commands do not reflect God's righteous and holy character because we cannot know God. His law is not based on His own character.

Because of that understanding of God, and the diminished view of how holy He is, it is obviously very hard for Muslims to understand how sinful we are, and the radical nature of human sinfulness. Many think that "'we all believe in the same God".

The Bible says that we fell in Adam: (Rom 5:12, I Cor. 15:22)

The New Testament makes it clear that there is a link between the sin of Adam and the sins of all mankind and this is found in the Old Testament as well (Ps 51:5)

Salvation

The Islamic view of salvation differs radically from the Christian view. Islam views sin as simple actions. When we witness to Muslims it is crucial that we share with them passages like the Sermon on the Mount to show that the biblical view of sin takes us much deeper into heart issues than just superficial actions. Basically, Islam claims that salvation is earned by good works; one of the images in the Quran is that of a scale. On the day of judgment, all your works will be weighed. Then those whose balance of good deeds is heavy, they will attain salvation: but those, whose balance is light, will be those who have lost their souls; in hell will they abide Sura 23:102-103.

Faith is important, but works are essential for salvation. There is hope of salvation, but no assurance, for them Christianity is a welfare religion. "Jesus paid it all". According to a Muslim, Christianity turns men into weak creatures who are helpless and hopeless and need a savior. Islam gives dignity to men. It says, you can do it. You can stand on your feet. This is basically the Islamic view of salvation. This view is reminiscent of Friedrich Nietzsche, who complained that the soft underbelly of Western Europe was the direct result of the "weakness of religion" propagated by

Christianity, which elevated virtues of mercy and grace rather than strength and courage, thus undermining the strength of the existential hero. We find this perspective also in modern existential heroes like Sartre and Camus and even in the popular writings of Ernest Hemmingway and others who complain that Christianity is for the weak and for those who have lost their humanity and have been emasculated.

The Death of Christ

Muslims deny both Jesus' death on the cross and His deity. They believe in Jesus and honor Him as a great prophet. The Quran mentions Jesus dozens of times and gives Jesus many honorary titles, for example, the messiah or Christ (Sura 4:157) and a sign (23:50) The Quran also claims that Jesus was born of the Virgin Mary. The Quran claims that Jesus worked many miracles, including raising people from the dead. Further, the Quran claims that Jesus is alive today, and according to Sunni Muslims, he will return before the resurrection of humankind to set the whole world straight.

Muslims assume that they already believe everything that needs to be believed about Jesus and that they already honor him as one of the greatest of Prophets, maybe second only to Muhammad.

In the Quran we read "That they (the Jews) said (in boast), we killed Christ Jesus, the son of Mary, the messenger of Allah. But they killed him not, nor crucified him but so it was made to appear to them, and those who differ therein are full of doubts with no knowledge but only conjecture to follow, for a surety they killed him not, nay, Allah raised him up unto himself (Sura 4:157-158). What ever happened, the Quran makes it very clear that Jesus never died on the cross.

However, it was made to appear to people as if Jesus had been crucified. Thus, God was involved in some kind of deceit to save the great honored prophet Jesus.

The Deity of Christ

Islam rejects not only the death of Christ on the cross and the doctrine of the atonement but also the deity of Christ.

The Quran says: "They do blaspheme who say: Allah is Christ, the son of Mary! But said Christ:" O Children of Israel! Worship Allah, my Lord and your Lord (Sura 5:72) Sura 5:75 9Sura 9:30)

When the rich young ruler asks Jesus "Good Teacher, what shall I do that I may inherit eternal life"? Jesus stops him in his tracks and says "Why do you call me good? No one is good but one, that is God" (Mark 10:17, 18). Some critics infer that Jesus is denying his goodness and his deity.

However, if He is denying his goodness, He is also denying His own sinlessness, which would disqualify him from offering an atonement. This inference flatly contradicts everything else Jesus said.

Let's examine what Jesus is saying here. The man who approached him had no idea that he was talking to God incarnate, and he probably had a very superficial understanding of goodness. He may have thought that all teachers or even all people were basically good. Jesus could have replied, "Your problem, Young man is that you have no idea what goodness is". Instead of saying that, Jesus points him directly to the law, the standard by which we are shown to be less than good.

He goes to the second table of the law. "You know the commandments:" Do not commit adultery," Do not murder, do not steal. The man replies," All these I have kept from my youth". He may have been thinking: "Is that all I have to do to get into heaven, Keep the Ten Commandments?" Jesus could have said, "Obviously, you were not there when I gave the Sermon on the Mount, when I explained what the real demands are within these commandments, or you wouldn't have made such a statement."

The Dark side of Islam

Is Islam a religion of peace or a religion of violence? Let us focus on the issue of Islamic justification for violence and terrorism. The violence of Islam has taken many forms. The vast majority of cases of persecution of Christians around the world today occur in the Islamic World. The Islamic law of apostasy states that any person who converts from Islam to any other religion, whether that person becomes a Christian, a Jew or whatever else, has committed a crime punishable by death.

Many people wrongly say that Islam is a religion of peace. Some claim that these violent Muslims are to Islam what the Ku Klux Klan is to Christianity. Mainly liberals and Muslims say that Osama bin Laden is to Islam what Timothy McVeigh was to Christianity. These are absolutely false analogies. Bin Laden could quote Quranic verses and traditions from Mohammad that justified his actions. McVeigh could not quote from the Bible or refer to Jesus to justify his actions. When the Klan commits acts of racial violence, they are betraying the teachings of Jesus Christ.

These false analogies and characterizations are being perpetuated by Western media, politicians and intellectuals.

Read (Sura 2:190-193), Sura 2: 216 (Sura 3:157-158) (Sura 3:169) Sura3:195, Sura 4:101, Sura 4: 89 (9:5), (9:29), Sura 5: 33 :8:12-13) Sura 47:4, Sura 9:14

These are not isolated passages that some people are misinterpreting or quoting out of context. Such verses are prevalent throughout the Quran, supporting the view that Allah wants his people to fight and destroy the enemies of the people of Allah by the use of the sword and other tools of violence.

Many people today say that these verses were intended just for the time of Muhammad, when the pagans of Mecca were attacking him, and that they do not apply today. However, not even once in the entire Quran is there a restriction put on these verses, which have been used throughout 1400 years of Islamic history, and these verses are universal for all times and all places.

In the Old Testament book of Joshua, God tells Joshua to destroy certain cities in the land of Canaan, but God specifically restricts His command to that time period for a special purpose and a specific group of people. Nowhere in the later Old Testament period do we read general commands to fight the pagans and spread the monotheistic faith of the Jews.

Some Muslims are fond of saying that the Jihad or holy war, in Islam is only a defensive action, only in case of self-defense are Muslims allowed to fight. Muslims are never allowed to initiate a war.

Islam divides the world into two segments: The House of Islam and the House of war. The goal of Islam is to dominate the world; the House of Islam must conquer the House of war.

In a sense it is similar to the Great commission of Jesus Christ; take the gospel to the ends of the earth. On the other hand, Muslims are ordered to use the sword to the ends of the earth.

Muslims do not believe only in the Quran as their ultimate source of authority. Some traditions and some sayings and actions of Muhammad are recorded in other books incorporated into an authoritative body of teaching for Muslims.

In the second century of the Islamic era, Ibn Ishaqe, a Muslim historian wrote a biography of Mohammad titled "Sirat Rasul Allah." It includes descriptions of the pattern of violence in the life of Muhammad and the example that he set for his followers in terms of violence.

Muhammad started his prophetic ministry when he was 40 years old, when he believed that he began to receive revelations from God. The first 13 years he preached in Mecca about the oneness of God and the pagan society rejected his message. He was invited to go to Medina. He became violent and political in Medina.

Muhammad ordered and orchestrated a series of assassinations against people who opposed him. The first person whom he had assassinated was an elderly Jewish man. In Medina 900 Jewish men were beheaded, and he took their women and children. On one occasion, Muhammad ordered the death of his own uncle, Abu Sufyan, who was the leader of an opposition group.

Besides the actions of Muhammad, another important thing that has shaped the Islamic legal system is the collection of Muhammad's sayings, the Hadith. In Sunni Islam this book is second in importance to the Quran.

The following saying is the basis of the law of apostasy in Islam: “whoever changed his Islamic religion, kill him”.

Chapter 14

The Biggest Holocaust in the History of the World finds no Place in History

The ethnic cleansing on the Indian sub-continent at the hands of the Arabs, Turks, Moguls, Iranians, and Afghans who occupied India for a period of 800 years, is not recognized by the outside world. The holocaust of the Hindus lasted 800 years. Historians and biographers of the invading armies and subsequent rulers of India have left detailed records of the atrocities they committed in their day-to-day encounters with India's Hindus.

Dr. Koenraad Elst in his Book "Negationism in India Concealing the Record of Islam" says "The Muslim conquests, down to the 16th century, were for the Hindus a pure struggle of life and death. Entire cities were burnt down and the populations massacred, with hundreds of thousands killed in every campaign, and similar numbers deported as slaves. Every new invader made his hills of Hindu skulls."

Thus, the conquest of Afghanistan in the year 1000 was followed by the annihilation of the Hindu population; the region is still called the Hindu Kush, i.e. Hindu slaughter. The Bahmani Sultans (1347 – 1480) in central India made it a rule to kill 100,000 captives in a single day, and many more on other occasions. The conquest of the Vijyanagar Empire in 1564 left the capital plus large areas of Karnataka depopulated. According to some calculations, the Indian subcontinent population decreased by eighty million between 1000 and 1525 (End of Delhi Sultanate.)

Will Durant write in his 1935 book "The Story of Civilization: Our Oriental Heritage" (page 459) "The Mohammedan conquest of India is probably the bloodiest story in history. The Islamic historians and scholars have recorded with great glee and pride the slaughter of Hindus, forced conversions, abduction of Hindu women and children to slave markets, and the destruction of temples carried out by the warriors of Islam during 800 AD to 1700 AD. Millions of Hindus were converted to Islam by sword during this period".

Francois Gautier in his book "Rewriting Indian History" (1996) wrote, "The massacres perpetuated by Muslims in India are unparalleled in history, bigger than the Holocaust of the Jews by the Nazis or the massacre of the Armenians by the Turks". Writers Fernand Braudel wrote in A History of Civilizations (1995), that Islamic rule in India as a "Colonial experiment, "was extremely evident and the Muslims could not rule the country except by systematic terror. Cruelty was the norm - burnings, summary executions, crucifixions or impalements, and inventive tortures. Hindu temples were destroyed to make way for mosques.

Irfan Hussain in his article "Demons from the Past" observes "While historical events should be judged in the context of their times, it cannot be denied that even in the bloody period of history, no mercy was shown to the Hindus unfortunate enough to be in the path of either the Arab conquerors of Sindh and South Punjab or the central Asians who swept in from Afghanistan. The Muslim heroes who figure larger than life in our history books committed some dreadful crimes. Mahmud of Ghazni, Qutb-ud-Din Aibak, Babbar, Mohammed Bin Qasim, and Sultan Mohammed Tughlak all have blood stained hands that the passage of years has not cleansed"

"Their temples were razed, their idols smashed, their women raped, their men killed or taken slaves. When Mahmud of Ghazni entered Somanath on one of his annual raids, he slaughtered all 50,000 inhabitants. Aibak killed and enslaved hundreds of thousands. The list of horrors is long and painful. These conquerors justified their deeds by claiming it was their religious duty to smite non-believers."

"Cloaking themselves in the banner of Islam, they claimed they were fighting for their faith when, in reality they were indulging in outright slaughter and pillage".

In pre- Islamic days, there were intense trade contacts between Indian and Arab pagans. They had pilgrimage exchanges also. The Hindus visiting Arabia paid their respects to the Arab sanctuaries, and considered the black stone in the Ka'aba as a Shiva lingam, a "Phallus of Siva". The Arabs, in turn, went to pray in the Somanath temple in Gujarat. The Muslims believed that the idols of the pagan goddesses Al-Lat and Manat (of The Satanic Verses fame) had been transferred to Somanath, and this is one reason why Muhammad Ghaznavi and other Muslim conquerors risked their lives in conducting raids deep into the territory in order to destroy the Somanath temple.

Timur was a Turkic conqueror and founder of the Timurid Dynasty. Timur's Indian campaign (1398 - 1399) AD was recorded in his memoirs collectively known as "Tuzk-i-Timuri". In them he vividly described probably the most gruesome act in the entire history of the world, where 100,000 Hindu prisoners of war in his camp were executed in a very short space of time. Timur, after taking advice from his entourage says in his memoirs. "They said that in the great day of battle these 100,000 prisoners could not be left with the baggage, and that it would be entirely opposed to the rules of war to set free these idolaters and foes of Islam. In fact, no other course remained but that of making them all food for the sword".

The Mogul emperor Babar who ruled India from 1526-1530 AD wrote a poem about killing Hindus:

"For the sake of Islam I became a wanderer,
I battled infidels and Hindus,
I determined to become a martyr
Thankful I became a killer of Non-Muslims".

The atrocities of the Mogul ruler Shahjahan who ruled India between1628 – 1658 AD are mentioned in the contemporary record called Badshah Nama, Qazinivi & Badshah Nama. He is the one who built the famous wonder of the world the Taj Mahal. The record states "when Shah Jahan was appointed Governor of Kabul, he carried on a ruthless war in the Hindu territory beyond Indus... The sword of Islam yielded a rich crop of converts. Most of the women burnt themselves to death. Those captured were distributed among Muslim mansabdaris (noblemen). The Afghan ruler Ahmad Shah Abdali attacked India in 1757 A.D and made his way to the holy Hindu city of Mathura, the Bethlehem of the Hindus and birth place of Krishna.

The atrocities that followed are recorded in the contemporary chronicles called, Tarik-I-Alamgiri. Abdala's soldiers would be paid 5 rupees (a sizable amount at that time) for every enemy head brought in. Every horseman had loaded up all his horses with the plundered property and atop of it rode the girl -captives and slaves. The several heads were tied up in rugs like bundles of grain and placed on the heads of the captives. Then the heads were stuck upon with lances and taken to the gates of the chief minister for payment. "It was an extraordinary display! Daily did this manner of slaughter and plundering proceed? And at night, the shrieks of the women captives who were being raped deafened the ears of the people. All those heads that had been cut off were built into pillows and the captive men upon whose heads those bloody bundles had been brought in were made to grind corn, and then their heads too were cut off. Those things did go on all the way to the city of Agra, or was any part of the country spared".

Division of India

The secular and leftist media and writers in India blame the British for the partition of India, but history will give you the correct answer. How many Muslim majority countries treat their minority population with dignity and equality? The answer is none. Muslims were responsible for demanding partition. We see the same behavior in the Middle East. The Palestinians do not want to co-exist with Israel. Their ultimate goal is to wipe out Israel from the map of the world. The division of India led to the displacement of millions of people, Hindus and Muslims who suddenly found themselves in different countries on August 15, 1947.

The partition killed more than one million innocent people and forced 10 million to flee across borders for safety. The Hindus of India were more tolerant, and they did not kill or expel all the Muslims of India. Today India is the second largest Muslim country in the world after Indonesia. Some calculations say that India may be the largest Islamic country in the world. Pakistan was established based on religion, but India became the largest secular democracy in the world.

The Muslim demands for a separate state in Pakistan and the area of Bengal, the former Pakistani region of Bangladesh, now an independent country, led to the greatest movement of refugees in the 20th century and 3 major wars between India and Pakistan.

Hindus in Pakistan

What happened to the Hindu minority in Pakistan? A situation many people do not care for. Prior to partition, 26% of the people in Pakistan were Hindus. Now there are less than 2%. But in India, Muslim birthrate is higher than that of Hindus. Writer, Fareed Zachariah, holds the view that in democratic societies like the United States, India and Israel, Muslims enjoy more civil and political rights than non-Muslims in Islamic countries, or in the so-called Islamic Republics.

The Pakistani constitution and legal system openly

discriminate against Hindus. During periods of tension and intermittent warfare between India and Pakistan, Hindus have been killed or expelled in large numbers. By contrast, Muslims in India have reached the highest positions of authority and prestige.

Four of them have been chosen as Presidents of India: Zakir Hussein (1967-1969), Mohammad Hidayatulla (1969), who was also Chief Justice, Fakhruddin Ali Ahmad, (1974-1977) and APG Abdul Kalam (2000-2007).

A 1965 law, "The Enemy Property Act" allowed Pakistani Muslim majority the legitimized confiscation of Hindu property. During 1970-1971, massacres were perpetrated upon Hindus by the Pakistani Army. Between 1989 and 1992, over 300 Hindu temples were destroyed by extremists. In 1971, East Pakistan became independent with India's help and was renamed Bangladesh, but they paid back in gratitude by killing large number of Hindus. Some estimate say 2-3 million people have been killed, the majority of them Hindus. It was one of the largest massacres in recent history, and one like the Iran - Iraq war that dragged on for 8 years (1980-1988).

Had the British left undivided India in 1947, the Muslim League would have continued its struggle for separate nationhood. With each riot, communalism would have deepened and could have led to the overthrow of secularism in India. We saw this in a microcosm in Yugoslavia when communism and autocracy ended. Civil war broke out, of course, because of Islam. Once the violence began, it could not be stopped. The Serbs, Croats, Bosnians went into hateful violence. Former Yugoslavia also created Macedonia

Kosovo and Montenegro. Civil war in India would have created multiple partitions as in Yugoslavia, instead of 2 states, India and Pakistan; civil war would have created 2 dozen countries with multiple disputes and bitter civil war memories. If someone blames Britain for division, it shows their lack of intelligence and knowledge about other peoples and nations.

Chapter 15

Holocaust of the Hindus of Kerala in South India

In recent times there has been a concerted and a well-orchestrated effort to distort and falsify recorded Indian history. The effort paints Great Britain as the ultimate villain in Indian history. Those who fought against the British are lionized; they are considered patriots and progressives in an effort to suit the selfish interest of a few.

One of these revisions relates to the invasion of Tipu Sultan of Mysore. Mysore under Tipu was a neighboring state of Kerala. The atrocities committed by Tipu in Kerala are facts of history, and yet there is a conspiracy to project Tipu as a national hero by suppressing, distorting and falsifying his crime against the innocent, largely non-Muslim, population of Kerala. Tipu's crime against humanity turned rivers of Kerala into rivers of blood. He offered non-Muslims only two choices: either convert or die, and many who refused to convert were put to the sword.

Tipu, however, was only a provincial despot, but on a national level, there are other villains like Aurangzeb, Nadir Shah, Mahmud Ghaznavi, Malik Kafue etc. In a sense, they were even worse in their own right, than Hitler and Mussolini.

However, coming back to Kerala, the brutalities that visited the poorly defended people of Kerala make the period of Tipu and his father Hyder Ali Khan from 1763-1792, the darkest period in the history of Kerala.

The Atrocities committed by Haider Ali Khan

The first serious resistance encountered by the invading army of Hyder Ali Khan was in Kadathanad. A broad picture of atrocities as described by a Muslim officer of the Mysore army in his diary and as edited by Prince Ghulam Muhammad, the 11th and only surviving son of Tipu Sultan is given below:

> "Nothing was to be seen on the roads for a distance of four leagues, nothing was found but only scattered limbs and mutilated bodies of Hindus. The country of Nair's (Hindus) was thrown into a general consternation which was much increased by the cruelty of the Mappilas (Muslims) who followed the invading cavalry of Hyder Ali Khan, and massacred all those who escaped, without sparing even women and children so that the army advancing under the conduct of this enraged multitude (Mappilas), instead of meeting with continued resistance, found village fortresses, temples and every habitable place

forsaken and deserted."

Hyder Ali dispatched his Brahmin messengers to woods and mountains, with the promise of pardon and mercy to the Hindus who had fled. However, as soon as the unfortunate Hindus returned on his promise, Hyder made sure that they were all hanged to death, and their wives and children reduced to slavery.

Tipu Sultan

After the death of his father in 1782, Hyder Ali's son Tipu Sultan became the King of Mysore. Tipu Sultan was a Muslim fanatic, and even more cruel and inhuman than his father.

Islamic Brutalities

According to the official report of Col. Fullerton of the British forces stationed in Mangalore, the worst type of brutalities on Brahmins were committed by Tipu Sultan in 1783, during the siege of the Palghat Fort, which was being defended by the Zamorin and his Hindu soldiers. "Tipu's soldiers daily exposed the heads of many Brahmins within sight from the fort for all to see. This act created terror and people accepted Islam to save their life.

Similarities between Tipu Sultan and ISIS of Iraq and Syria

One thing has never changed in the history of Islam. Mohammad and his followers beheaded thousands of people and displayed their heads to create terror. All Islamic conquerors have practiced the method of beheading. In 2014 the Islamic State or (ISIS) grabbed large areas of Iraq and Syria declaring a cross border caliphate. Tens of thousands of people have been beheaded or shot to death. The victims were Shia Muslims, Christians, Kurds and other minority sects. Even two years old children have been beheaded. ISIS soldiers reportedly were playing soccer or (football) with chopped heads of men in the playground. So we still experience the 7th century Islam in the 21st century. In Iraq ISIS soldiers rounded up Shia teenage boys, while they were pleading and sobbing for mercy, ISIS shot and killed all those young boys. ISIS records these events with advanced digital technology to show the whole world the brutal killings and create terror in the hearts of the people around the world. Kozhikode, formerly, Calicut, in Kerala was a center of Brahmins. There were 7000 Namboodiri homes, of which more than 2000 were destroyed. Tipu did not spare even women and children. Hindus were forcibly circumcised and forced to eat beef.

The war that Tipu Sultan waged in Kerala was a cruel Islamic war against the Hindu population, mainly for conversion of Hindus by force. Yet there are many naive Hindus in Kerala who admire Tipu Sultan as a hero. Atrocities committed in Malabar during the days of Tipu Sultan's military regime have been described in great detail in the famous works of many reputed authors. Notable among them were Travancore State Manual of T.K. Velu Pillai and Kerala Sahitya Charitam of Ulloor Parameshwara Iyer.

Noted historian K.M. Panicker chanced upon Tipu's correspondence at the India Office Library in London. They have since been published. "Over 12,000 Hindus were honored with Islam. Local Hindus should be brought before you and then converted to Islam."

In a letter (December 14, 1788) Tipu said to his Army

Commander in Calicut, "You should capture and kill all Hindus. Those below 20 years may be kept in prison and 5000 from the rest should be killed hanging from treetops." Writing on January 14, 1790, to Badroos Saman Khan, he said "I have achieved a great victory recently in Malabar and over four Lakh (400,000) Hindus were converted to Islam". Tipu issued orders in different parts of Malabar "All means, truth or falsehood, fraud or force should be employed to affect their (Hindu) universal conversion to Islam."

Fr. Bartolomaco, a Portuguese traveler and historian wrote a book in 1790 titled, "Voyage to East Indies. "In it, he wrote "First there was a corps of 30,000 barbarians who butchered everybody on the way, followed by the hired gun unit under the French Commander, M. Lally. Tipu was riding on an elephant behind which another army of 30,000 soldiers marched. Most of the men and women were hanged in Calicut; first mothers were hanged with their children tied to necks of mothers. The great Barbarian Tipu Sultan tied the naked Christians and Hindus to the legs of elephants and made the elephants to move around till the bodies of the helpless victims were torn to pieces. Temples and Churches were ordered to be burned down, desecrated and destroyed. Christian and Hindu women were forced to marry Mohammadans and similarly their men were forced to marry Mohammadan women. Those Christians who refused to be honored with Islam were ordered to be killed by hanging immediately. These atrocities were told to me by the victims of Tipu Sultan who escaped from the clutches of his army and reached Alappuzha, which is the center of the Carmichael Christian mission".

Destruction of Hindu Temple

According to the Malabar Manual of William Logan, who was the District Collector for some time, Trichambaram and Thalipparampu temples in Chirackal Taluk, Thiruvangattu Temple (Brass Pagoda) in Tellicherry, and Ponmeri Temple near Vadakara were all destroyed by Tipu sultan. The Malabar Manual mentions that the Maniyoor mosque was once a Hindu temple.

Tipu Sultan and Christians

The invasion of Tipu Sultan is called "Padayottam" in Kerala.

The ancient Christians of India were known as Christians of St. Thomas. They are also known as Syrian Christians, since they have been using Syriac for liturgical purposes with or without a mixture of Malayalam, the language of the people of the State of Kerala, also called Malabar In olden days.

Anyone born into a Kerala Syrian Christian family is generally known as a Syrian Christian or Nasrani (Nasrani is a Semitic term that refers to the inhabitants of Nasira or Nazareth) in Israel. The English term is "Nazarenes"). Syriac Christianity is a culturally and linguistically distinct community within Eastern Christianity.

To understand what effect the invasion of Kerala by Hyder Ali and his son Tipu Sultan had on the Syrian Christian community, one needs only to study the timeline of events between 1766 and 1790 in Kerala.

Tipu's soldiers did great damage to several Christian Churches and Seminaries that they encountered in Kerala. Tipu's soldiers razed the old Syrian Christian Seminary in Angamally to the ground. Many churches in Malabar and Cochin were damaged as well. The Syrian Christian community had to flee to Calicut. Tipu Sultan's army set fire to the church at Palayoor and attacked the Ollur church in 1790.

When Tipu Sultan invaded Guruvayur and the adjacent areas, looting temples and churches, a large number of refugees came to Kunnamkulam headed by Pulikkottil Joseph Kathanar, Vicar of Arthatt church.

The biggest loss to the Syrian Christian community was not the damage done to their institutions alone, but the indiscriminate destruction of coconut, Arecanut, pepper, and cashew Plantations by the Mysoreans when they swept through Kerala. Most of the Syrian Christians were prosperous with large land holdings.

References:

1. Malabar Manual by William Logan.
2. Tipu Sultan as known in Kerala by Ravi Varma.
3. Voyage to East Indies by Fra Bartolommeo (Portuguese traveler and historian)
4. History of Kerala by A. Sreedhara Menon.
5. Cochin State Manual by C.A. Achuta Menon.
6. State Manual of Travancore by T.K. Velu Pillai.
7. Tipu Sultan X – rayed by Dr. I.M. Muthanna Usha Press Mysore 1980.
8. Freedom Struggle in Kerala by Sardar K.M. Panicker.

Some 50 historians have tried to rewrite history and make Tipu a Patriot, but they don't have intellectual honesty and a clear and objective sense of history. Anywhere Islam went, people were converted by force. Today the Indian Sub-

Continent has around 500 million Muslims. Their ancestors were not converted by preaching the life of Mohammad or the loving principles of Allah. In conclusion, what happened in North India and the rest of the world happened in Kerala too.

Mappila Peasant Revolt (A Muslim in Malabar is known as Mappila)

Sardar K.M. Panicker and other Communist and Islamic historians are in a joint mission to legitimize and glorify past brutal Islamic atrocities against Hindus. These atrocities in Malabar, which took place during a period around 1921, are being classified as a part of the Freedom struggle and Peasant movement - against feudal lords. Here also the shaky historians blame the British, as usual. The textbooks also glorify the Jihadist terrorists as freedom fighters. Certainly at that time, feudal lords around the world indeed subjugated ordinary people, but in Malabar the Muslim religion played a major role similar in Jihadist revolts, just as it did in other parts of the world for the last 1400 years.

Khilafat Movement

The Mappila rebellion is an offshoot of the Khilafat Movement. The Mappilas were a band of Muslim fanatics who were the descendants of the Arabs who settled in Malabar, Kerala, in about the 8th and 9th century AD. They mostly married native Indian wives. They were responsible for 35 outbreaks during the British rule.

During the early months of 1921, excitement spread speedily from mosque to mosque and village to village. All throughout July and August, Khilafat meetings were held in which the "The Karachi resolution" was fervently endorsed. Knives, swords, and other weapons were secretly manufactured and preparations were made to proclaim the coming of the Kingdom of Islam.

Government property was destroyed, Europeans were murdered, and Mappilas declared independence from foreign rule. A man named Ali Musliar was proclaimed Raja (King), and Khilafat flags were flown. Massacres, forced conversions, raping of women, and the desecration of temples were perpetrated. By the end of 1921, the British suppressed the rebellion.

Atrocities by Mappilas

One tragic incident took place on the barren hillside between Thuvoor and Karuvayakandi in north Kerala, at a well. On August 24, 1921, Chambrassery Imbichi Koithangal along with 4000 of his followers, had organized a massive rally under the solitary tree on the hillside and watched forty people who cowered before him, their hands tied behind their backs. All of them were Hindus. The charges against them were read in public. According to the mob, these Hindus had conspired with the army against the Muslims. Thirty-three of the Hindus were given death sentences, and the first 3 were shot to death immediately. The rest were taken to the nearby well one after the other, like lambs to a slaughter house.

The executioners stood near the well and each of the Hindus was made to bend while being held down. Then an axe man started to chop their heads and afterwards their bodies were thrown in the wells. Some of them did not die immediately, but were thrown into the well mortally wounded. Those who survived the fall were to die a slow agonizing death among the bloody corpses. Three days after the blood bath, people could hear cries from the well, but were too terrified to help. More than 2500 Hindus including men, women and children, all perished there.

About thirty thousand Hindus were forcibly converted to Islam. The conversion ceremony included mandatory eating of beef by the new converts. 200,000 Hindus had to flee from their homes. The Marxist government. lead by EMS Namboothiripadu in 1957 twisted and distorted the history by classifying the Mappila riot as a part of the freedom movement, and offered pension to those who participated in the revolt. **These historians followed the command of Karl Marx. Marx declared "The first battlefield is the re-writing of History"**

Chapter 16

Islamic Negationism

The Muslim world universally denies the Holocaust and they believe that it is a Zionist propaganda. Haj Mohammed Effendi Amir el- Husseini (1897-1974), the Grant Mufti of Jerusalem went to Germany and made a pact with Hitler. He recruited Muslims from Bosnia and provided a Muslim division for the Allied Forces in the 2nd World War. He believed in the power of socialism and that the State was the ultimate source of power and truth. The evil has never disappeared, but it is still continuing in different forms. Communism was evil to the core, and Ronald Reagan destroyed Soviet Union and weakened Communism. After the decline of Communism, Islamo- fascists are growing rapidly in more than sixty countries in the world.

Mass Murder

Most of the Jews were gassed in concentration camps. The Jews of Europe reached the camps by rail. The trains- sometimes fifty cattle Cars long, were packed with exhausted men, women and children, who had been traveling many days without anything to eat or drink. Some died during the journey; many more were killed immediately upon arrival. Not all the "Pieces" as the SS called the victims, could be killed at once, so families in the rear cars waited in ignorance on the tracks outside the train station for the front cars to be "unloaded". The whole murderous process from getting off the train to being turned into ashes and dumped in a nearby river often took no more than a few hours.

Hitler's efficient and smart system was described by the Commander of Auschwitz, Rudolf Hess, not long before he was hanged for his crimes: "The Jewish prisoners were made to undress near the bunker after they had been told that they had to go into the room in order to be deloused. All the rooms – there were five of them- were filled at the same time; the gas proof doors were then screwed tight and the contents of the gas containers discharged into the rooms through special vents. After half an hour, the doors were reopened; there were two doors in each room. The dead bodies were then taken out and brought to pits in small trolleys, which ran on rails. Those too ill to be brought to gas chambers where shot in the back of the neck. "Louis L. Snyder, Hitler and Nazism (New York, Bantam1, 1967 PP.30-31)"

One key to the death – camp system was sheer speed. The moment the Jews got off the train they were surrounded by armed guards yelling at them to keep moving.

The faster the process, the less chance there was for panic or rioting. The Nazis were brutally calculating; any revolt would force a bloody massacre right there on the train platform – costing precious time in clean up.

Perhaps even more important than speed was deception. The camp administrators went to great lengths to deceive the prisoners until the very last moment, sure in the knowledge that few could foresee what lay in store. The Nazis knew how to prey on the psychology of their vulnerable prisoners. In Claude Lanzmann's remarkable Holocaust documentary "Shoah", survivor Fillip Muller describes how the Nazis inspired false hope among the Jews in the camp, even as they were being led to their death.
"It was obvious that hope flared in those people", he remembered. "You could feel it clearly". (IBID PP 64-70)
Muller recalled the horrific moment when the German executioners gathered a group of prisoners in the crematorium courtyard. Grabner spoke up; "we need masons, electricians, all the trades". Next, Hossler took over. He pointed to a short man in the crowd. I can still see him. "What is your trade"? The man said: Mr. Officer, I'm a tailor", "A tailor? What kind of a tailor" "A man's ... no, for both men and women"? "Wonderful; we need people like you in our workshops". Then he questioned a woman; "what's your trade? "Nurse", she replied. "Splendid"! We need nurses in our hospitals, for our soldiers. We need all of you! But first, undress, you must be disinfected. We want you healthy".
I could see the people were calmer, reassured by what they were told, and began to undress. Even if they still had their doubts, if you want to live, you must hope. Their clothing remained in the courtyard, scattered everywhere. Aumeyer was beaming, very proud of how he'd handled things. He

turned to some of his German Secret Service men and told them "you see! That's the way to do it" IBID PP 64-70.

Even this deception extended to the gassing process: "As people reached the crematorium, they saw everything – this horribly violent scene. The whole area was ringed with SS guards with machine guns. They were mainly Polish Jews; they had misgivings; they knew something was seriously amiss, but none of them had the faintest of notions that in three or four hours they'd be reduced to ashes. When they reached the "undressing room", they saw that it looked like an International Information Center! On the walls were hooks, and each hook had a number. Beneath the hooks were wooden benches. So people could undress "more comfortably", it was said. And on the numerous pillars that held up this underground "undressing room", there were signs with slogans in several languages: "Clean is good"! Lice can kill"! "Wash yourself"! to the disinfection area". All those signs were there only to lure people already undressed, into the gas chambers. And to the left, at a right angle was the gas chamber with its massive door.

In crematorium 2 and 3, zyklon gas crystals were poured in through the ceiling, by the so – called SS Disinfection Squad, and in crematoriums 4 and 5, through side openings. With five or six canisters of gas they could kill around two thousand people. The Disinfection Squad arrived in a truck marked with a Red Cross sign and escorted people along, to make them believe they were being led to take a bath." IBID PD. 124.

Franz Suchomel, a Nazi SS officer at the Treblinka camp, said "you must remember, it had to go fast. And the

Blue Squad also had the task of leading the sick and the aged to the" infirmary", so as to not delay the flow of people to the gas chambers. Old people would have slowed it down. Assignment to the "infirmary" was decided by Germans. Old women, sick children, children whose mothers were sick or whose grandmother was very old, were sent along with the grandma, because she did not know about the "infirmary". It had a white flag with a red cross. A passage led to it until they reached the end. They saw nothing. Then they'd see the dead in the pit. They were forced to strip and sit on a sand bank, and were killed with a shot in the neck. They fell into the pit. There was always a fire in the pit with rubbish paper and gasoline. People burnt very well." (I BID 14 pages 119-120).

Now the 21st century Hitler of Iran, Ahmadinejad, says that the Holocaust was a hoax and never happened.
The Nazi bureaucrats, were responsible for seizing the wealth of the victims – from their real estate and bank accounts right down to their jewelry and luggage. Nothing "useful" was wasted from the hair on their heads to the gold in their teeth; It all went to the Nazi coffers.

One especially chilling detail involves the Nazis use of portable gas chambers, or gas vans to kill their occupants with carbon monoxide. After noticing that the victims rushed en masse to the rear door trying to escape the gas, Nazi officials reacted by shortening the trucks by 3 feet, in order to avoid damaging their rear axles. In letters at the time, the victims are described as "merchandise"; for the Nazis, evidently, thinking of their victims as dry goods rather than human beings, only helped make the process more efficient. I BID 15. Page 104

Nearly 70% of the European Jews were slaughtered in these camps during the war, and millions of other human beings with them-men, women, children and babies. However, it did not happen overnight. To kill millions of people in the midst of their functioning societies, the Nazis needed a system, a plan devised by bureaucrats and executed by efficient men who had analyzed all the difficulties of managing the "task" and who worked diligently to refine the "process".

A Tale of Lies

As documents from the Nazi era reveal, the efficiency of the genocide was also abated by virulent anti-Semitic propaganda which demonized the victims and glorified the Nazi murderers. The Jews were depicted as members of "an international conspiracy against National Socialist Germany, who operated as parasites on society, extracting society's resources for their covetous benefit. They were lesser human beings, whose extermination would benefit society as a whole. Joseph Goebbels, one of the most influential members of the Nazi regime wrote that there were good and bad humans. The fact that the Jews still live amongst us is not proof that he is one of us; (no more than the flea's domestic residents makes him a domestic animal. (Joachim remarks in the Nazi Years. Page 155)

Even while waging war in 1941, Goebbels kept up his public excoriation of the Jewish people. He wrote "Every Jew is a sworn enemy of the German people." Every German soldier's death in this war is the Jew's responsibility. Jews had no claim to equal rights and they should be silenced whenever they want to open their mouths. Even if a Jew should perform an act of kindness towards them, he warned his readers not to be fooled- and to punish him in return with contempt."

Communism and Totalitarianism: The Evil Twins

Totalitarian States are breeding grounds for evil. The satanic evil of a Nazi Germany, or a Soviet Union, can survive only under a totalitarian system, where dissent is outlawed. Nazi movement was not only against the Jews, but it virulently opposed the tenets of Christianity. It was in thrall to the Philosopher Friedrich Nietzsche's vision of a "Superman", which was built on the belief that Aryans were superhuman and Jews non-humans. Nietzsche had famously declared that "God is dead", and the leaders of the Third Reich saw that, without God, the state and its leaders were free to shape morality for themselves.

Nietzsche, whom the Nazis could quote on demand, had written that for the average citizen "there is no such thing as the right to live, the right to work, or the right to be happy! In this respect man is no different from the meanest worm". The superman, on the other hand, Nietzsche exalted as a "beast of prey", a magnificent blond brute, avidly rampant for spoil and victory". William L. Shirer, <u>the rise and fall of the Third Reich</u> P100.

Adolf Hitler Hated Christians and Jews.

Liberal historians place Nazism and Communism as two extreme ends of the ideological spectrum – far right and far left. But in truth, these two totalitarian models are actually very similar. Both were avowedly socialistic and both established the state as god.

The visionary leader of Great Britain, Winston Churchill, reorganized the dangerous folly of Prime Minister Chamberlain's position. Churchill said "we have sustained a defeat without a war" and do not suppose that this is the end. This is only the beginning of the reckoning. This is only the first sip, the first foretaste of a bitter cup. Remark – The Nazi years P 40. His prediction became true within a short period of time. How did Churchill see what Chamberlain had missed? Each man had access to the same information about Hitler and Nazi Germany. Chamberlain and Churchill had entirely different views of human nature. Churchill knew evil when he saw it.

Modern day American leftists are the true descendants of Neville Chamberlain. They are naive and lack critical thinking. Hollywood liberals, Jimmy Carter and modern Democratic leaders are" useful idiots" for our enemies. Leftists all over the world throughout the ages think alike, but a correct and unprejudiced historical knowledge an unravel the puzzle and complexity.

Chapter 17

Is the Bible Corrupted?

Islam invented a vaccine to immunize Muslims to prevent conversion to Christianity. Christianity converted millions of people around the globe over the centuries. Only Islam prevented mass conversion to Christianity. The name of the vaccine is called "The Bible is corrupted" Since the quran is a forgery of the Bible with great twists Muslims have been brainwashed from childhood with this deception. If you look the statistics, Muslim conversion to Christianity is very minimal.

Christians are thrown off guard by Muslim's claim that the Bible has been changed. The quran recognizes the prophets as divinely inspired, and their words as the very word of God. The quran recognizes all the old testaments prophets and recognizes the Taraut (the Law), the Zabur (the psalms) and the injils (the Gospels) as the word of God. When you challenge the Muslims to read the Bible, they will say "Jews and Christians changed the Bible. "Why do Muslims believe the Bible was changed even though there is no evidence of any such change in the thousands of ancient manuscripts available to all for research.?

History gives the correct answer

Although the quran in Sura 6:34; 10:34 says that no one can change the word of God, the Bible and the Koran do not agree. The Bible and the Koran differ widely on fundamental concepts of faith and practice.

Since the Bible existed before the Koran the burden of proof is upon the Muslim to prove that the Bible is incorrect, and that the Koran is correct. The Bible was completed 500 years before the Koran was revealed to Muhammad. If I write a book that contradicts a historical document written at the time of American Independence, it is incumbent upon me to prove the older document was false and the facts in my present book is accurate. The document written at the time of independence would not have to prove itself against a latter document. This is not logical, rational or true to the principles of the science of history. Merely repeating without real facts that the older document was not accurate, does not by default mean the newer document is true. It must stand on its own and prove itself.

The answer is found in history. The Bible was not translated into Arabic until after the ninth century, and so the author of the Koran did not have access to it. For example, the great Islamic scholars of the medieval period, including Ali al-Tabari, Amr al-Ghakhiz, Bukhari, and Al-Mas'udi all accepted the same New Testament text we accept today.

It was only after the Bible had been translated into Arabic that Islamic scholars were able to compare the Koran with the Bible. Only then does the idea that Bible had been corrupted and falsified begin to appear. In 1064, Ibn-Khazem first charged that the Bible had been corrupted and the Bible falsified. He made this charge not on the basis of any evidence. He did so in an attempt to defend Islam against Christianity because he was among the first to realize the contradictions between the Bible and the Koran. Believing, by faith that the Koran was true, the Bible must then be false. He said, "Since the Koran must be true it must be the conflicting Gospel texts that are false. But Muhammad tells us to respect the Gospel. Therefore, the present text must have been falsified by the Christians after the time of Muhammad."

Islamic Allegation #1:
The Bible has changed or altered over time

Christians have a firm foundation for confidence in the unchanging text of both Testaments. Not only is there a super-abundance of more than 5,664 Greek manuscripts from which the original wording of New Testament books can be determined; there are also 18,000 other manuscripts in several other languages, e.g., Armenian, Latin Vulgate, Ethiopic, and more.

It is rare for secular books of antiquity to have as many as even a dozen ancient manuscripts. Typically, their best copies date about 700-1000 years after the date of composition. By contrast, there are complete papyrus manuscripts of many entire New Testament books that date from a mere 100 years after the originals. One papyrus scrap

of John 18 has been dated to as early as 115 A.D., just 25 years after John was written!
Sir Frederic Kenyon, former director of the British Museum, said that..."In no other case is the interval of time between the composition of the book and the date of the earliest manuscripts so short as in that of the New Testament."
Based on his findings, he concluded: "The last foundation for any doubt that the scriptures have come down to us substantially as they were written has now been removed."

Islamic Allegation #2:
The Jews have changed or "concealed" portions of the Torah (Old Testament)

This charge of "change," sometimes called "harrafa," is extremely far-fetched. It flies in the face of clear evidence from the Dead Sea Scrolls, discovered in 1948. Before 1948, the oldest complete Hebrew manuscript dated to 900 A.D. The Dead Sea discoveries brought shocking news. A complete scroll of Isaiah was found, which is dated to about 100 B.C. With one stroke, we leaped 1000 years deeper into the past, in terms of the oldest known copy of Isaiah!

It gets interesting at this point, since scholars can see how well the Masoretic copiers had preserved the Old Testament text. As scholars compared the two Isaiah texts (from 900 A.D. & 100 B.C.), they were startled by the precision of copying.

Isaiah 53, for example, has 166 words, and there are only 17 letters that differ. Ten are just spelling differences. Four are "minor stylistic changes, such as conjunctions." The three remaining letters that differ are the word "light,"

added in verse 11, which does not affect the meaning.
As Geisler and Nix pointed out, "Thus in one chapter of 166 words, there is only one word (three letters) in question after a thousand years of transmission—and this word does not significantly change the meaning of the passage." [For further reading, see: What is the importance of the Dead Sea Scrolls? (ChristianAnswers.Net)] What's more, many dozens of verses in the Qur'an allude to the fact that the true "Torah" was not distorted; it was in the possession of John the Baptist, Mary, Jesus, and His disciples. "According to the Qur'an, God or Muhammad under God's orders, appealed to the Torah and the Gospel more than 20 times... Muhammad asks the Jews to bring the Torah to settle a dispute. People 'read' the Torah and the Gospel which are 'with them'."[3]

Islamic Allegation #3:
Contradictions and Biblical discrepancies undermine any confidence in the Bible

Finally, Muslims point out so-called contradictions between parallel verses, such as when genealogies of the same lineage diverge, or when numbers of people in census lists do not correspond, or when the parallel accounts in the synoptic gospels differ slightly.

A few of the Old Testament numerical discrepancies are in all likelihood due to inadvertent copyist errors. On the other hand, most "discrepancies" of substance are easily handled by employing exegetical common sense.
For example, it actually enhances the credibility of Biblical accounts (such as the synoptic parallels) when slightly different patterns of facts are described. If they were just "invented" (possibly in collusion) or "copied," there would be no difference at all!

History of the English Translation

The Textus Receptus is the Greek text that Erasmus, the famous Renaissance scholar, published in A.D. 1516. It was the first New Testament Greek text ever published. The basis for the Textus Receptus was three minuscule, three cursive manuscripts that Erasmus had before him. One was copied in the tenth century, the second was copied in the twelfth century, and the third, the one he mainly relied upon, was copied in the fifteenth century. The Textus Receptus became the standard Greek text for over three hundred years. It contained this changed reading in Revelation 22:14, "Blessed are they that do his commandments".

Since 1516 the world of scholarship and archeology has discovered thousands of earlier Greek texts. The great uncials that were copied from the very beginning when the books of the New Testament were first gathered into one, have been discovered since Erasmus. An uncial is a Greek text written in large, square capital letters. We have thousands of Greek manuscripts written cursively. They are called minuscule. The writing of uncials with big, square letters was slow and difficult. In the seventh century, a way was invented to write cursively, as you write longhand in English, writing in a running hand. After the seventh century all of the manuscripts were written in that cursive style. There are thousands of Greek minuscule.

Enumeration of Greek New Testament manuscripts. This list was compiled in 1967 by Kurt Aland:

Papyri	81
Majuscules	267
Minuscule	2,764

Lectionaries	2,143
Total	5,255

There are presently 5,687 Greek manuscripts in existence today for the New Testament.

There are thousands more New Testament Greek manuscripts than any other ancient writing. The internal consistency of the New Testament documents is about 99.5% textually pure. That is an amazing accuracy. In addition, there are over 19,000 copies in the Syrian, Latin, Coptic, and Aramaic languages. The total supporting New Testament manuscript base is over 24,000. This is an astonishing and an amazing total when you remember there is only one manuscript of the annals of Tacitus, the great Roman historian. There is only one manuscript of the Greek anthology. So much of the literature of the ancient world of Plato, Sophocles and Euripides would depend upon one or two manuscripts. By comparing those thousands of manuscripts, you can see where a scribe emended the text here, where he wrote a little explanation of the text there, where he changed a word here. Essentially, practically, doctrinally, for all worship purposes, for our own reading and edification, the King James Version, the Authorized Version, and the Textus Receptus is superlative. But once in a while you will see where a scribe has made a change, has interpolated, has emended, has (what he thought) corrected. These emendations are most apparent and are not a part of the word of God.

Throughout the Koran a diligent student can see contradictions and poor literary quality. Muslims are happy to criticize the Bible however, at the same time they don't want any scrutiny of the Koran.

Abrogated Verses in the Koran

There are some peaceful verses in the Koran. However, the violent and hateful versus have abrogated them. The Koran itself explains what to do with conflicting verses. If two passages conflict, the one written later is better than the one written earlier. The earlier passage has been abrogated by the later one. All the peaceful versus were written earlier, and intolerant, hateful and violent verses were written later. Now you know why ISIS and other Islamic groups kill non-Muslims.

There are as many as 225 versus of the Koran that are altered by later verses. This is called "Abrogation". Of the Koran's 114 Suras, only 43 are without abrogated verses.

Different versions of the Koran

Muslim source materials indicate that at least four different versions of the Koran existed before the political leader ordered to have them burned. (Al-Tamhid 2.247). The four versions were written by people who knew Muhammad in person. Each person created their unique version of the Koran. The differences were serious enough to cause one Muslim group to call another group heretic, so a political decision was made to have only one Koran. When Muhammad died in 632 AD, the Koran had not been recorded and collected into a book. Instead, Muslims memorized large portions of the Koran. The Koran means to recite.

The original Koran was completed in 634 AD, during the political reign of Abu Bakr.

Since all the other copies of the Koran were burned, what was wrong with them? Certainly, the Koran of today is not the original Koran recorded only 2 years after

Muhammad died. Problems for the Koran began during the reign of the third political leader of Islam, whose name was Uthman (644-656) It appears that as the Islamic faith spread with military conquest across a large area, the soldiers were reading different versions of the Koran. So Caliph Uthman ordered four men to rewrite the manuscripts in perfect copies from the Hafsa codex. Having completed a new version Uthman ordered all other Korans to be destroyed by fire.

SATANIC VERSES IN THE KORAN?

This section is taken from www.beholdthebeast.com
A time came in Islamic history when the Muslims faced severe persecution from the unyielding Meccans, so severe in fact, that eighty-three of Muhammad's followers had to flee to Abyssinia (Ethiopia). When the persecution grew worse, Muhammad underwent a moment of despair and made compromising "revelations." He declared the possibility of Allah having a wife, Al-Lat and two daughters, Al-Uzza and Manat, as recorded in Surat an-Najim:

"For truly did he see, the signs of his Lord, the greatest! Have ye seen Lat, and Uzza, and another, the third [*goddess*] Manat? What! For you the male sex, and for him, the female? Behold, such would be indeed a division most unfair!" (Sura 53:18-22).

This indirect confession of polytheism made the Meccan pagans happy. Their bone of contention had been done away with (earlier, he had fearlessly lashed out against polytheism). The Meccans immediately lifted the boycott, stopped the persecution, and peace again reigned in Mecca. The Muslims who had migrated to Ethiopia heard the good news and returned home. But by then, Muhammad had withdrawn his confession. It appears that Muhammad realized the far reaching negative effect his compromise with the polytheists would have on his ministry. So on at least this one occasion, he admitted that he was actually inspired by Satan, as we read in Surat al-Hajj: "Never did we send an Apostle or a prophet before thee but when he frames a

desire, Satan threw some [*vanity*] into his desire. But God will cancel anything [*vain*] that Satan throws in.
And God will confirm [*and establish*] his signs. For God is full of knowledge and wisdom, that he may make the suggestions thrown in by Satan, but a trial. For those in whose hearts is a disease and who are hardened of heart: Verily the wrong doers are in a schism far [*from truth*]" (Surat al-Hajj 22:52,53).

The Al-Jalalayn interpretation is that after Muhammad recited Surat an-Najim (Sura 53) before a Council, the angel Gabriel informed him that the verses *were put in his tongue by Satan*. Muhammad felt sorry and confessed his mistakes, supposing a similar fate befell preceding apostles.
Later on Allah annulled these Satanic verses with better "revelations." As the last part of verse 53 suggests, Allah supposedly permitted Satanic utterances to be in the Koran to test weak Muslims or to cut off those who had hardened hearts. Thus, Islam itself regards Sura 53:18-22 to be Satanic, and Muhammad did indeed reject them later. Remember Salman Rushdie? He didn't invent those Satanic verses. Those Satanic verses are really in the Koran.

Here is a serious point for Muslims to ponder:

So, provably, there was one occasion when Muhammad was unable to tell the difference between the voice of Satan and the voice of Allah. Is that the only time it happened? Could there be other revelations believed to be from Allah that were really from Satan? Is it possible that the whole Koran is little more than Satanic verses? Muslims claim that the Koran contains the words of Allah, 100%, but the Koran not only has Satanic verses, but also a demonic Sura. Unbelievably, a whole Sura (chapter) in the Koran is named after the demons.

Shocking but true. Sura 72 is entitled Jinn (demons), Here is a short quote:

"1. Say: It has been revealed to me that a company of Jinns listened [*to the Koran*] They said, we have really heard a wonderful Recital!

2. It gives guidance to the right, and we have believed therein we shall not join [*in worship*] any [*gods*] with our Lord.

3. And exalted is the majesty of our Lord: He has taken neither a wife nor a son.

4. There are some foolish ones among us who used to utter extravagant lies against God.

5. But we do think that no man or spirit should say aught that is untrue against God.6. True, there were persons among mankind who took shelter with persons among the jinns but they increased them in folly.

7. And they [came to] think as ye thought, that God would not raise up anyone [*to judgement*].

8. And we pried into the secret of heaven: but we found it filled with stern guards and flaming fires.

9. We used, indeed, to sit there in [*hidden*] stations, to [*steal*] a hearing: but any who listen now will find a flaming fire watching him in ambush.

10. And we understand not whether it is intended to those on earth or whether their Lord [*really*] intends to guide them to right conduct.

11. There are among us that are righteous and some the contrary: we follow divergent path.

12. But we think that we can by no means frustrate God, throughout the earth, nor can we frustrate Him by flight.

13. And as for us, since we have listened to the guidance, we have accepted it: and any who believes in his Lord has no fear, either of a short [*account*] or of any injustice.
14. Amongst us are some that submit their wills [*to God*] and some that swerve from justice. Now those who submit their wills-they sought out [*the path*] of right conduct.
15. But those who swerve, they are [*but*] fuel for hell fire." It should disturb every Muslim that demonic conversations are considered to be part of the supposed word of Allah. But upon reflection you can see how and why they are.

First of all, let us define Jinns.

Advanced Learners Dictionary of Current English defined jinns to be genies or goblins - mischievous demons - ugly looking evil spirits. The Bible defines demons as angels who followed Satan in his rebellion against God:

And there was war in heaven: Michael and his angels fought against the dragon; and the dragon fought and his angels, and prevailed not: neither was their place found anymore in heaven. And the great dragon was cast out, that old serpent, called the Devil, and Satan which deceiveth the whole world; he was cast out into the earth and his angels were cast out with him. (Rev.12:7-9)

No one should take a jinn's claim seriously, that "some of them are righteous," Sura 72:11. Satan is the father of lies (John 19:44), so why should we believe what his Jinns said in the Koran? Jinns, like their master (Satan), are liars. To deceive us, they gather half-baked truths into bundles of lies. That demons and Satan are barred from the true heaven forever is indicated from their own confession in verses 8-9.

There they admit that they unsuccessfully tried to storm heaven but met opposition from stern-looking angelic guards. Even their attempt to spy at heaven was foiled as they admit in verse 9. The true nature and root of Islam is revealed in verse 14 when the jinns, (whom the Bible God cast out of heaven) became Muslims and found a refuge in Islam.
"Among us [*jinns-demons*] are some that submit wills (to God) [*i.e. Muslims*] and some that swerve from justice. Now those who submit their wills [*demonic Muslims*] they sought out [*the? path*] of right conduct." (Sura 72, Jinn, 14).

God forbid that I should belong to the same religion that the arch-enemies of God, the demons, also profess. Who could sponsor a religion? that includes God's arch-enemies, i.e. the jinns (demons)? Only Satan posing as Allah would do so. Before their conversion, the evil spirits confessed what was later to be a central theme of Islam, that Allah has neither taken a wife nor had a son (72:3).

It is clear at this point that while posing as the angel Gabriel and claiming to be from Allah, one of these jinns (demons), gave Muhammad a denial of the sonship of Christ and the fatherhood of God. This blatant falsehood is repeated over twenty times in the Koran. Bearing in mind the Satanic verses incident, one must acknowledge that the devil can impersonate a holy angel. (2 Corinthians 11:13-15). As an interesting note, when Muhammad received his first "revelations," he was not sure of the source of them himself. His wife (Khadija) convinced him that they must have come by the angelGabriel.1Muhammad's encounter with the jinns (demons) is also recorded in another Sura, Sura 46, Al-Ahqaf, 29-32: 29: "Behold, we turned towards the company of jinns

[*quietly*] listening to the Koran; when they stood in thy presence thereof, they said "Listen in silence!" when the (reading) was finished, they returned to their people, to warn [*them of their sins*].
30: They said, O our people! we have heard a Book revealed after Moses, confirming what came before it: It guides [*men*] to the truth and to straight Path.

---

1 See Yusuf Ali's Commentary No. 31-33.

But you don't have to dig very deep to find the truth. Even a cursory reading of the Qur'an is sufficient to prove that it is a fraud. There is no way the creator of the universe wrote a book devoid of context, without chronology or intelligent transitions. Such a creative spirit wouldn't need to plagiarize. He would know history and science and thus wouldn't have made such a fool of himself. The God who created man wouldn't deceive him or lead him to hell as Allah does. Nor would he order men to terrorize, mutilate, rob, enslave,
and slaughter the followers of other Scriptures he claims he revealed, wiping them out to the last. One doesn't need a scholastic review of the Qur'anic textto disprove its veracity. It destroys itself quite nicely.

APPENDICES

Appendix 1

Myths about the Israeli-Arab conflict (1)
Is "Occupation" the cause of this conflict?
From ("Flame" published by NewsMax on September 2006)

In the decades in which the Israeli-Arab conflict has raged, certain myths have been repeated so often and so insistently by Arab propaganda that most of the world has come to believe them. Today, we briefly examine one of those myths. What are the facts?

The myth of "Occupation" being the cause of conflict.

The very concept of occupation, as applied to Gaza and Judea and Samaria (the "West Bank"), is a myth. When the Egyptians were in possession of Gaza for almost 20 years nobody accused them of being occupiers. The Jordanians, who were in possession of Judea/Samaria (the" West Bank") and much of Jerusalem for the same length of time, were not considered occupiers by the nations of the world and by the inhabitants of the area. The Israelis were considered "occupiers" when, after a war of extermination against them, they prevailed and came into possessions of these territories. The oldest rule of warfare is that to the victor belong the spoils. Do people expect France to return Alsace-Lorraine to Germany? Do they expect the Czech Republic or Poland to return the German territories awarded to them after Germany's defeat in World War II? Of course not!

Those countries evicted most of the original inhabitants or caused them to flee. Israel, in contrast, has never evicted a single Arab from these territories. On the contrary, lured by the prosperity the Israelis have created, tens of thousands of Arabs from adjacent Syria and Jordan have come to live there.

Israel's "occupation" of those territories is a myth.

But even so, the hope that Israel's abandonment of any territory - the same old "land-for-peace" formula - would bring about peace is an illusion and a fallacy. In order to establish peaceful relations with its northern neighbor Lebanon, Israel abandoned the security zone of southern Lebanon. But instead of acknowledgment and gratitude, the result has been never -ending attacks with Katyusha rockets, led by Hezbollah, the "army of God", which is supported and incited by Iran and by Syria. It makes life on Israel's northern frontier almost unbearable. Israel, unilaterally, and in order to appease the Palestinians, the United States, and world opinion, vacated Gaza and evicted thousands of Israeli families and abandoned their homes, institutions, extensive agricultural installations, and valuable infrastructure. Not a single Israeli citizen, not a single Israeli soldier, remains in Gaza. But, in the few months since it has abandoned that territory, Israel has been provoked to bloody warfare and has been subjected to daily attacks by Qassam rockets. It is only a matter of time until one of those devices will crash into a school or into a hospital causing untold casualties and destroying vital infrastructure.

Destruction and civil war.

Instead of using their newly won "liberty from occupation," the Gazans have engaged in what is practically a bloody civil war and have destroyed most of their meager infrastructure. They have demolished and vandalized the valuable and extensive greenhouse installations that the Israelis had created, which could have been the basis for a prosperous agricultural economy and of substantial export income. But they focus their efforts and their energy on digging tunnels under the wall that separates them from Israel, in order to attack Israeli military, killing and kidnapping their soldiers and thus bringing added misery upon themselves. Having the disastrous examples of the withdrawal from the southern Lebanon security zone and now from Gaza, it is easy to imagine what would happen if Israel would not have learned from experience and - under pressure from the U.S. and world opinion - would commit the folly of abandoning Judea/Samaria (the "West Bank"). While Gaza is isolated surrounded by Israel and the sea, the "West Bank" is connected to Syria and Jordan. Within days of Israel's abandonment of that territory, Syrian tanks, Syrian aircraft, Syrian artillery, and Syrian and perhaps even Iranian troops would be stationed on the ridges of the Judean hills that dominate Israel's heartland. That heartland is only nine miles wide at its narrow waist. Israel’s population centers, Israel's military installations, Israel's industrial capacity, Israel's utilities, and Israel's international airport would be in the gunfights of the Arabs, sworn to the destruction of Israel. The attack against Israel, the hoped-for final assault against the hated Jews, would begin within days or weeks and might

well be successful.
The Palestinians, along with most other Arabs and Moslems, are single-mindedly focused on the destruction of Israel, to "wipe it off the map." If Israel were pressured into ending the "occupation" of the territories, it would not bring peace. On the contrary, it would bring about bloody warfare, just as in Gaza and Lebanon, and could well be the end of Israel. Those who advocate the ending of the "occupation" do so either out of ignorance or because they have a death wish for Israel. Those who advocate the ending of the "occupation" do so either out of ignorance wish for Israel.

APPENDIX II

ISIS AND THE MAPPILA REBELLION OF MALABAR

I shudder when I look at those lurid videos of the killings of innocents by ISIS a la "Islamic Justice." I cannot feel indifferent to the killings; for me, they are not remote happenings to some strangers in some far away land. Such killings are part of my own story, part of my family history as narrated to me by my grandmother who lived through it all, some 93 years ago, in 1921. It is the story of the Mappila Rebellion of Malabar, an offshoot of the Khilaphat movement in which atrocities were committed on Hindus and other non-Muslim communities, out of revenge and hostility, fueled by a seventh century ideology. There is a close parallel between the Khilaphat Rebellion of 1921 in Malabar and today's frightening specter of ISIS atrocities in Iraq and Syria. Reasons for the atrocities vary somewhat, but the main purpose was the same: the establishment of a Caliphate.

My grandmother's narrative was chilling. The murderous mob from Ernad Taluk (part of today's Malappuram District) forded the shallow end of the Chaliyar and went, swords in hand, from door to door, looking for non- Muslim families. They dragged men, women, and children out of their homes, raped women, maimed and murdered the men who refused to convert, and carried away the children after putting fire to their homes. My grandmother told me that I almost missed being born, but now I am here to relate the story, because, she told me, she was protected by a friendly Muslim family that shielded her and her two daughters when the marauders came calling. The Chaliyar, she told me, had turned crimson and the headless bodies bobbed their way down to the Arabian Sea. When the local police force could not put down the rebellion, a special police force called MSP (Malabar Special Police) was formed. But even they could hardly contain the fury of the mob. Finally, the local British Administration had to call in the army and the formidable Goorkha Regiment. Between them, they destroyed the rebels, thousands were killed or imprisoned, and hundreds were banished to the Andaman Islands.

The Mappila Rebellion was part of the Khilaphat Movement of India, which in turn was part of the Pan-Islamic program inaugurated by the Ottoman Emperor of Turkey. Gandhi was implicated in the movement at the start, for Gandhi took it as part of the "Swaraj" movement. Later, Gandhi withdrew his support of the movement and allegedly left the beleaguered Hindu and Christian communities to the mercy of the violent mob of Mappilas. A prominent Nair leader, C. Sankaran Nair wrote a scathing criticism of Gandhi whom he called an 'anarchist'. "The horrid tragedy," he wrote, "continued for months; thousands of Mohammadans were killed or wounded by the troops; thousands of Hindus were butchered by the raging Mappila mobs; women were subjected to shameless indignities, hundreds of them threw themselves into wells to avoid dishonor or forced conversion." .... "This is what Malabar owes to the Khilaphat agitation and to Mahatma Gandhi."

In pop culture, the events of the Mappila Rebellion were featured in novels and Malayalam language films. Renowned author Urub's "Sundarikalum Sundaranmarum" was set in a backdrop of the Malabar uprising. The novel features thirty characters of three generations of eight families in Malabar. The book won the Keraliya Sahitya Academy Award and numerous other awards. In 1988, a Malayalam Language film, Aayirathi Thollayirathi Irupathonnu (1921) directed by I.V. Sasi, written by T. Damodaran Nair, and starred in by Mammootty and Madhu, depicts the events of the Mappila Rebellion. The film won the Kerala State Film Award.

In 1924, Mustafa Kemal Ataturk had overthrown the Ottoman rule in Turkey and established a pro-Western Republic. He had also abolished the rule of the Caliph. Ever since, there have been several attempts to restore the position of the Caliph as the religious head of the world Muslim community. The efforts had collapsed as there was no way to bring about reconciliation between the feuding groups of Muslims who pronounce fatwa against each other and consider each other apostates or 'kafirs'. So just as in the rebellion in Malabar, ISIS, for all its formidable strength, may also be headed for abject failure. Powerful Muslim states themselves are at loggerheads with Abu Bakr al-Baghdadi and his murderous minions.

So what is ISIS, and who is its reclusive leader? ISIS, acronym for "Islamic State of Iraq and Syria" is a mediaeval outfit that has imposed the most brutal form of the Sharia Law throughout its territory. They have destroyed Shiite mosques and tombs, massacred those whom they deem infidels, imposed stringent restrictions on women, banned music, dancing, and smoking, and drinking. ISIS is the most media-savvy militant group to emerge in the Middle East.

The commander-in-chief of ISIS is Abu Bakr al-Baghdadi, the man who has declared himself Caliph of the Islamic world. Baghdadi is an Islamic scholar, poet, and Sunni extremist; an enigma to his own followers as well as to his enemies. Baghdadi started as a preacher of the Salafic wing of Islam, a hardline militant group a la Osama Bin Laden. His goal is to restore the Caliphate and crown himself as the Caliph. His method of reaching that goal has been inspired by the four immediate successors of Muhammad in spreading Islam by the sword. He models his justice system after the system used by the Abbasid Dynasty of Caliphs– using beheadings, stoning, and crucifixion. He uses terrorism as a way to avenge humiliation, subjugation, and subordination at the hands of infidels, as he stated in July, 2014.

At informal discussions, I am often asked about the difference between Christianity and Islam. I tell them, there is no simple answer to that question. Books can be written about the differences. However, for a simple answer, I would say, Christianity was born of love and forgiveness; Islam, of war and violence. Christianity had its bad days (Middle Ages) and Islam had its good days, but as Hasan Suroor wrote in Hindu (Sept 29, 2014), Christianity got over its violent history, but Islam failed to move on and update its theological precepts. Dedicated Christian scholars and theologians work hard at Biblical analysis and criticism to unearth the true message of the Sacred Books. They use modern methods of studying the original languages of the Bible and Biblical archeology. Few such efforts are reported from the Islamic side. So the ideology that drives these terrorist groups are not based on any deep understanding or research into their sacred scripts. They are, apparently, based on blind faith.

Joseph Devaprasad

Appendix III

WRESTLING WITH CONTRADICTIONS

I was focused, for the last couple of weeks, on a special topic: Islam. Islamic faith has never been a strange phenomenon to me. I lived among 'the believers' for almost two decades. In my younger days the difference between 'them' and 'us' was defined by our separate identities, rituals, and symbolisms. I recognized 'Mappilas' by their peculiar attire: checkered 'mundu' with its ends knitted together; long, loose kurta and a turban carelessly knotted; men shaved their heads and grew long beards, smelled bad, for they never used deodorants; men washed themselves every time they urinated – I still remember watching curiously from my brother's riverside restaurant, a sickly old man hurrying down to the river holding the large growth at his scrotum(hydrocele) to wash himself clean of the urine.

Women were recognized by their loose coveralls which shielded them from gawkers and gave them an air of modesty, but they evidently roused curiosity as they seemed to wear little or no underclothes. Our next door neighbor was a Muslim who was called 'Haji' as he had been on a 'haj' to Mecca with his wife. They were some of the nicest people I knew when I was young. The Haji brought fruits and other goodies to our Onam celebrations; they visited us whenever we were home for holidays and invited us to their home. On one such occasion, the lady suggested that I convert to Islam and marry one of her daughters. As I mentioned in my last piece, it was their ancestors who had protected my grandmother from being put to the sword by the murderous mob that came across the river looking for non-Muslims to convert or to kill during the infamous 'Mappila Rebellion' of Malabar. Later on, when I was a young man, my grandmother used to narrate the story of her ordeal to me, and I remember her protectors gratefully. But ironically, she warned me not to trust Muslims as "they were liars and cheats and had no qualm about hurting those who were not of their faith." Later, while reading V.S. Naipaul's account of life in his native Trinidad, I read the same advice given to him by his father. So to my adolescent sensibility, this apparent contradiction in Islam was disturbing, and I wanted to get to the root of this and many other seeming contradictions in the Muslim way of life.

My quest for the root of the many contradictions in Islam led me all the way to the seventh century Arabia, to the time and teachings of their prophet. For my quest, I largely relied on two books, besides the Islamic scriptures themselves: The books were "Infidel" by Ayaan Hirsi Ali and "The Truth About Muhammad" by Robert Spencer. "Infidel" was the book of the month that we discussed at our book club meeting, on October 8, 2014 at St. Vincent de Paul parish hall. The club consists of 12 members, most of whom, retired, and all of whom are American. I am the only one with a different skin tone, but I moderated the exchange as I had read the book twice and I had recommended it for our book of the month. It was a heated session, an eye opener to almost all and they were grateful to me for bringing the book to their attention.

Ayaan Ali was born in Somalia in 1969, grew up in Somalia, Saudi Arabia, in Ethiopia and Kenya. She went to Europe as a refugee in 1992, and became a member of parliament in Holland. She made a movie with Theo Van

Gogh, a descendent of the Famed Van Gogh, the artist. The movie focused on the abysmal life of women in many Islamic countries. Theo Van Gogh was murdered in broad daylight, in November, 2004, on a street in Amsterdam by a Moroccan Muslim who stuck a warning to Ayaan on Theo's chest, with a dagger. Ayaan came to the United States in 2006 and now lives in Washington D.C with "body guards and armored cars." She works for a Think Tank in the D.C. area, and part time, at Harvard. One of the blurbs on the book cover says: "A brave and elegant figure, an honest woman. No one who reads her memoir will doubt the self-questioning and the rigorous honesty of her mind." The book will tell you the atrocities she and numerous other women have suffered in some Islamic lands, how women are flogged for committing adultery; how they are forced into marriages with older men whom they loathed; how they are beaten by their husbands on a regular basis and how they are shunted by their fathers when they are raped by a relative, and sometimes put to death. The book also will tell you in graphic detail how little girls are tied down and subjected to the inhuman practice of clitorectomy and sewed up for life with the approval of imams. "In Saudi Arabia where Islam is practiced in its purest form, every step we (women) took is infused with concepts of purity or sinning, and with fear. Wishful thinking about the peaceful tolerance in Islam cannot interpret away this reality: hands are still cut off, women still stoned and enslaved just as the prophet Muhammad decided centuries ago."

The second book that helped me to identify contradictions in Islam is "The Truth about Muhammad" by Robert Spencer. The book was a New York Times best seller when it was published in 2006. Spencer is the director of Jihad Watch, a program of the David Horowitz' Freedom

Center. "At a time," writes Daniel Pipes, "when even in the West, the pious narrative of Muhammad has gained a near hegemonic hold; Robert Spencer offers a rare skeptical biography and the interpretation of the prophet of Islam. Relying exclusively on Islamic sources, 'The Truth About Muhammad' argues that, for fourteen hundred years the 'words and deeds of Muhammad have been moving Muslims to commit acts of violence.'' Spencer's book offers a wealth of information on the man and his teaching that conquered much of the Arab world and spread the Islamic faith throughout the Middle East and far beyond.

I did not pick these volumes for their authors' fierce criticism of Islam, but for their integrity and their fearless honesty. I am a professing, practicing Catholic. Criticizing and, much less, denigrating other people's religion are not among my Church's agenda. I attend Mass every day; I visit four churches and listen to homilies and sermons; but never have I seen or heard attempts to put down other cultures or other religions. We are exhorted to love every human on the face of the planet and pray for them and help them in their needs. Such sermons are based on the principle that God created all men, even the terrorists who point their guns at us; God loves them too; He has a plan for them; He wishes their good. So who am I to hate, to pass judgment, to condemn!
Why should my heart ache, my eyes weep, my soul sink? Whenever I see a perfect stranger hurt, sick, lonely or abandoned because every time I try to ignore other people's problems or pain, something stirs deep within me and rekindles an inner light. There's contradiction when a religion is defined as a religion of peace, but in practice, spreads violence and hatred!!!

Joseph Devaprasad

The above notes were taken from the following books.

God's War on Terror by Walid Shoebat with Joel Richardson

The sword of the prophet by serge Trifkovic

Islam prophesied in Genesis by Dennis Avi Lipkin

Answering Islam by Norman Geisler and Abdal Saleeb

Return to Mecca by Dennis Avi Lipkin

The Great Divide. The failure of Islam and the Triumph of the West. By Marvin Olasky.

The Road to Holocaust by Hal Lindsey

The Truth about Muhammad by Robert Spencer.

The Dark Side of Islam by R.C. Sproul and Abdul Saleeb

Why we want to kill you. By Walid Shoebat.

Behind the Veil by Abd EL Schafi

The History of Islam by Robert Payne.

Unholy War by Randall Price

Unveiling Islam by Ergun Meh Mechmet Caner and Emir Feth Caner

Islam 4th edition by Caesar Farah

The Glorious Qur'an Translation by Mohammed Pickthall

The Qur'an Translated by M.H. Shakir.

The Islamic Invasion by Robert Morey

Nagationism in India By Koenraad Elst

Infidel by Ayaan Hirsi Ali

A God Who Hates. By Wafa Sultan

They must be stopped. By Brigitte Gabriel

Because They Hate. By Brigitte Gabriel

Understanding the Hadith by Ram Swarup

Hadith of Bukhari Volumes 1, 11,111& 1V

Conspiracy by Daniel Pipes

Real enemies' conspiracy Theories world war 1 to 9/11 By Kathryn s. Olmsted.

Behind the Veil by Abd EL Schafi

The Everlasting Hatred by Hal Lindsey

Unveiling Islam by Ergun Meh Mechmet Caner and Emir Feth Caner

Islam 4th edition by Caesar Farah

Race & Economics. Walter E. Williams. Hoover Institution Press. Stanford University. California.

In the Shadow of the Sword. By Tom Holland.

Made in the USA
Columbia, SC
31 January 2025

52609130R00137